Angels Long to Look

Gospel Encounters with Jesus

D. Marion Clark

Angels Long to Look © 2021 by D. Marion Clark
All rights reserved.

Scripture texts introducing each chapter are from ESV Bible ® (The Holy Bible, English Standard Version ®). Copyright © 2001 by Crossway Bibles, a publishing ministry of Good News Publishers. Used by permission. All rights reserved.

ISBN: 978-1-956597-00-4 (paperback), 978-1-956597-01-1 (epub)

Publishing and Design Services: MelindaMartin.me

Printed in the United States of America

To DAVID, JOANNA, FIN, and COLE.

I long to look into your stories

that you will have with your Savior.

Contents

Part One: The Word Became Flesh 1

    The Angel of the Annunciation 3

    Elizabeth 9

    Zechariah 15

    The Shepherd 21

    Mary 25

    Anna 31

    The Wise Man 37

    Joseph 43

Part Two: And Dwelt Among Us 49

    The Angel in the Wilderness 51

    The Servant at the Wedding in Cana 57

    The Woman at the Well 63

    The Leper 69

    The Paralytic 75

    The Invalid at the Pool 81

    The Centurion of Capernaum 87

    John the Baptist 93

    Simon the Pharisee 99

    The Prostitute 105

    A Disciple in the Storm 111

    The Pig Herdsman 117

    Jairus 123

    The Woman with the Discharge 129

    The Boy with the Fish 135

    Peter on the Water 141

    The Canaanite Woman 147

    The Half-Believing Father 153

The Man Born Blind	159
Martha	165
The Lawyer	171
The Pharisee	177
The Rich, Young Ruler	183
Zacchaeus	189
Nathaniel at Jesus' Triumphant Entry	195
Mary, the Sister of Martha	201

Part Three: Christ Died ... 207

The Angel in the Garden	209
Nathaniel in the Garden	213
Malchus	219
Pilate	225
Simon of Cyrene	231
The Centurion at the Cross	237
John after the Crucifixion	243
Joseph of Arimathea	249
Nicodemus	255

Part Four: He Was Raised ... 261

The Angel at the Tomb	263
Mary Magdalene	267
Cleopas	273
Thomas	279
Peter	285
Matthew	291

Conclusion: He Was Lifted on High ... 297

The Angel of the Ascension	299

Concerning this salvation, the prophets who prophesied about the grace that was to be yours searched and inquired carefully, inquiring what person or time the Spirit of Christ in them was indicating when he predicted the sufferings of Christ and the subsequent glories. It was revealed to them that they were serving not themselves but you, in the things that have now been announced to you through those who preached the good news to you by the Holy Spirit sent from heaven, things into which angels long to look.

—1 Peter 1:10–12

PART ONE

THE WORD BECAME FLESH

The story has begun. What has been foretold is now unfolding. To me was given the privilege to announce the birth of the Messiah, the Son of David, the Son of God. I carried out my duty with joy… and with trembling.

My first message was for the old priest Zechariah. Only once in a lifetime is a country priest allowed to offer incense to the Lord inside the temple. Even then one is chosen by lot and many miss out. But my Master made arrangements for that day. His good fortune had been appointed, not so much to make the offering but to receive my message.

I frightened him. We angels always do frighten humans. We don't mean to, mind you. I don't know if it is the surprise (no footsteps to hear) or something about our appearance. Well, anyhow, there he was half scared out of his wits. Maybe that is the reason he reacted the way he did when I gave him the good news that he and Elizabeth would have a baby. He had prayed every day for a child, I think more for his wife's sake than his own. Barrenness is difficult, especially for the woman. I say he was praying, but he was probably no different from most people who pray for something for a long time. After a while it becomes just something to do. The hope, the expectation of an answer dies out.

That, no doubt, was the case with Zechariah. When I told him his prayer had been heard, he wouldn't believe me. He wanted evidence. Now, I consider myself a patient angel. I realize Zechariah was just being human, but really, I am an angel. It is not as if a mere man was giving him the news. Wasn't my presence alone enough proof for him? I stand in the presence of God. Let me see him try to do that. Isaiah learned what it is like. And here is this little priest questioning if I knew what I was saying. I gave him

The Angel of the Annunciation

In the sixth month the angel Gabriel was sent from God to a city of Galilee named Nazareth, to a virgin betrothed to a man whose name was Joseph, of the house of David. And the virgin's name was Mary. And he came to her and said, "Greetings, O favored one, the Lord is with you!"

—Luke 1:26–28

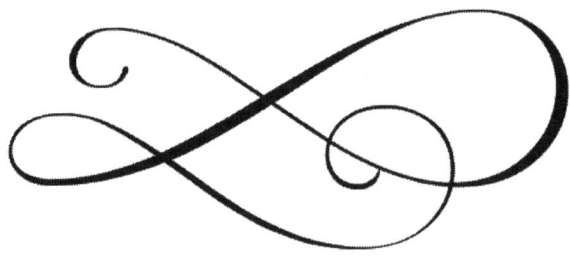

For full story:
Luke 1:5–23; 26–38; 2:8–14

evidence, all right. He would not speak again until he saw his baby. It may have seemed a harsh sentence, but at least it got my message across.

My second message was to Mary, a sweet young girl. This assignment was different for me. I've been sent to deliver special messages before, but this one...well, even I was shaken. To tell this maiden that she would bear the Holy One of God was as overwhelming for me to tell as it was for her to hear. Usually I say first my "fear not" routine, because I realize the person is awed at seeing me. But it was my turn to be awed, and I blurted out, "Greetings, O favored one, the Lord is with you!"

Her troubled expression put me back to my senses, and I remembered that I was speaking to a mortal human. I encouraged her not to be afraid and then delivered the message I was sent to give about the Messiah, the Son of God, that she was to bear. She did not doubt like Zechariah, and she asked a good question about how she would bear a child when she had yet to be married. It saved what could have been a serious misunderstanding. I've noticed that humans like to take things into their own hands, all because they think they must figure out for God how to carry out his assignment. Sarah was that way. Where did she get the idea that God needed Hagar to keep his promise to her for a child? What if Mary had assumed that she should quickly get pregnant by Joseph or someone else? Then she would have had a mess on her hands!

She showed much wisdom with that question, but it was her final word that will always leave the deepest impression on me: "Behold, I am the servant of the Lord; let it be to me according to your word." An angel could not have spoken more fittingly. Where did this mortal, this young girl get such a trusting, faithful spirit? I cannot think of any woman, or man, for that matter, who responded with the faith that she did. Not Sarah, nor Abraham. Not Moses. Mary could not know how this mystery would unfold. Surely she had to be aware of the embarrassment to come. "Let it be to me." These human beings can sometimes surprise.

The third message was the most fun to deliver. I had shepherds to go to, and this time the Lord let the fullness of his glory be displayed through me. Yes! I am invisible for a moment. The shepherds are having a quiet night. A couple of them are yawning and about to nod off, and then, Pow! I suddenly appear with an intense light all about me. That woke them up! Again, I said the old line, "Fear not," but, hah, how could they not be? Even I have to admit I was a bit terrifying clothed in the glory of the Lord.

I told them the greatest news that anyone had ever heard before.

"I bring you good news of great joy that will be for all the people. For unto you is born this day in the city of David a Savior, who is Christ the Lord. And this will be a sign for you: you will find a baby wrapped in swaddling cloths and lying in a manger."

And then—this was the great touch—a whole company of angels appeared with me. Not a few. Try to imagine thousands of angels like me suddenly appearing and shouting praise to God. I assure you, the shepherds did not forget that experience. They all fell on their knees quaking. They had to cover their ears. Then, as suddenly as the company had appeared around me, they disappeared. I stayed a moment longer, then vanished.

Yes, it's a good story, but I have one more visit to tell of. I went to that stable too and looked upon the little infant, and it unnerved me. I could have used someone to tell me not to be afraid.

You see, that infant is the glorious Lord in whose presence that I told Zechariah I stood. He is the God whom I have worshiped since my own creation and whose commands I obey. And it unsettles me to see him like the humans whom my very presence frightened.

This is my King? Why is he doing the work of a servant? He is the Head of the army of all the heavenly angels. Why is he now placed in a helpless state? Why become a mere man lower than I? Why, even for human standards, is his arrival so humble?

I was there when poor Isaiah was brought into the presence of the holy God. I pitied him in his fear. But in the presence of the little baby dressed in rags of cloth, I know now such fear. I know what it is like to think I know God, only to be thrust into the presence of a God more mysterious than I could ever imagine—the eternal begotten Son of God born anew in the flesh of his own creatures.

And for what purpose? For what purpose has he given up his place of glory? I have longed to look deeper into the prophecies of God's prophets. And now they have begun to unfold. What is next? What will my Lord do now dressed as one lower than my own kind? I know that it means something wondrous. As I said to Mary, "He will be great and will be called the Son of the Most High. And the Lord God will give to him the throne of his father David, and he will reign over the house of Jacob forever, and of his kingdom there will be no end."

That is a journey back up to glory. But I can perceive enough to know that suffering somehow lies in this infant's destiny, this infant for whom all the legions of angels are prepared to defend. Already he has emptied himself of his heavenly glory. Already he has stooped to take on the flesh of man. Still, suffering for the Lord of glory? How can this be? Or more to the question: why should it be? What love is it that compels such a giving up by the Father? What is the joy that is set before the Son to travel such a path? We angels wait with suspense to see what will unfold.

So, the story begins.

Elizabeth

After these days his wife Elizabeth conceived, and for five months she kept herself hidden, saying, "Thus the Lord has done for me in the days when he looked on me, to take away my reproach among people."

—Luke 1:24–25

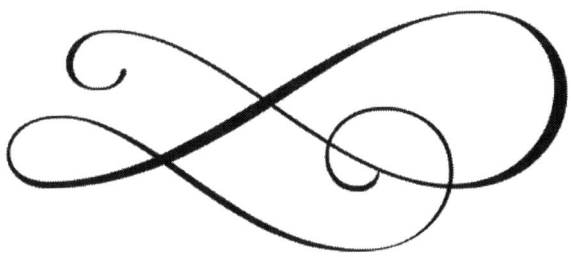

For full story:
Luke 1:24–25; 39–45

I laughed. Yes, just like Sarah, I laughed when Zechariah communicated to me what the angel had said. (I would have said "told," but then my husband could not speak.) I laughed for the same reason as Sarah. I am old, beyond the years of childbearing. The idea of me bearing a child was plain silly…and painful to suggest. It only drew out again the sorrow of disappointment that my old age had finally succeeded in burying.

I never felt anger against God. He is the sovereign Lord. He may give as he pleases and withhold as he pleases. Blessed be the name of the Lord. But the emptiness of the womb cannot but be felt as the emptiness of the soul. It is different for a man. He desires a child, in particular a son, through which to pass on his name and typically his land. We are Levites. We have no land of our own. The Lord is our inheritance.

But I am a woman. It is not for a name that I desire a child but for the very child himself. To bear life, to raise that life, to hold that life in my arms—that has always been my deep desire. From the first night of marriage, I eagerly anticipated the joy of bearing a quiverful of children. Did the Lord not say through the prophet Malachi that he brought a man and woman into union so that he could have holy offspring? Surely he knew my heart's desire to produce such fruit.

And yet I know that it is not the destiny for every woman. There are those who have never been taken in marriage. There are others barren like me, even who have conceived but have miscarried. There are others who have given birth only to lose a child young. And there are those who have had the joy of children only for those children to bring shame in later years.

We live in a fallen world, as my good husband has reminded me many times. Like Hannah's husband, he would add, "Am I not more to you than ten sons?" I suppose he thought that since such words were in Scripture they must be good to say. They were as little comforting to me as, I'm sure, they were to Hannah.

My barrenness—it has been a reproach among my people. There were no words spoken to me, no direct words. Even so, I knew the thoughts. Is there unrevealed sin? The Lord knows all. Poor Zechariah. To be a priest with a barren wife. He puts on a brave face.

And now, here I am with child. I have only now come out of hiding, feeling assured that he will come to birth. Thus the Lord has done for me in the days when he looked on me, to take away my reproach among people. Truly nothing is impossible with God. And, as if the gift of a child were not enough, the angel of the Lord said that he is to be great before the Lord. Already we know that he is to be a son. We even know his name—John.

How is he to be great? The angel said that John will turn many of the children of Israel to the Lord their God. It seems that my son will bring a revival to our land. We need it. Is not the very occupation of Rome God's judgment for our sins? He will turn the hearts of the fathers to the children, and the disobedient to the wisdom of the just. He will lead our people to repentance.

But more. He is to make the people ready for the coming of the Lord—the Messiah. The time has come! After generations of waiting, of hoping, of pleading, the time for the Anointed One is upon us. My son will be like Elijah, making way for the Lord's coming.

Who will the Anointed One be? How will he come? Straight from heaven? More likely a birth. Then who will be the mother? Has she already given birth? What is she like? Is she like me, long past the age of bearing and yet now a miraculous conception? Is she excited? Is she frightened? Does she know whom she bears?

So many questions, I know, but I have had time to do much thinking, and the more thinking I do the more questions I have. We Jews have waited for so long, so long that the Messiah's coming is unreal. We have not thought through what it would be like in real life. He is just supposed to show up.

That he might have a mother and a father, that he would have to grow up—those are not the types of things we have considered.

But now that I am with child with the forerunner of the coming Lord, such thoughts come to me, and I cannot but think of her, the mother. Is she from a wealthy family, a distinguished family? What of her husband? Is he a priest like Zechariah? That would seem right, but then, no, Zechariah says the Scriptures reveal that the Messiah would come from the house of David of Judah. He will be a king.

And then, will we ever know him? Zechariah and I are old. Can we even expect to see our own son grown? What will he be like? Will it be as a priest that he carries out his calling? How strange it seems to be told so much and yet know so little. John will prepare the way of the Lord by calling our people to repentance. I expect then that he will become great in the kingdom that the Messiah ushers in. Perhaps he will be at the Lord's right hand. How I pray that I will see that day. Perhaps I will stand beside the mother of the Anointed One, and together we will beam with pride and joy at our two sons.

Well, I should not get too caught up with the future. It is the present that matters, and I must prepare for my child's birth. Even now he is being formed by God. As King David wrote:

> For you formed my inward parts;
>   you knitted me together in my mother's womb.
> I praise you, for I am fearfully and wonderfully made.
> Wonderful are your works;
>   my soul knows it very well.

Yes, wonderful are your works, O God! I feel the knitting being done. I feel the kick of your child in my womb, and I praise you for the fearfully and wonderfully made son.

I must prepare a good home for him. He will know love from the moment he is born. I will make sure of that. I must see that he gets his proper nourishment. Will I be able to provide his milk with my old body? The Lord, no doubt, will see to it. He can do anything.

O Lord, give me strength and health to raise my son, to be always there for my son. And when the time comes to give him up, grant me the strength to do so willingly. He is to go forth in the spirit of Elijah, but to me he is my Samuel—a gift from the Lord. As long as he lives, he is lent to the Lord. Someday, he will leave to go to whatever place you have prepared for him. Is it to be the temple? Where else better to call our people to repentance?

I pray for the Messiah's mother. Prepare her, as well, for the birth of her child. Prepare us both for whatever sacrifices we must make. We know that it matters not what happens to us. All that matters is for us to be good mothers to our sons.

My heart is glad, feeling my son safe within my womb. Still, I cannot shake off some anxiety as to what will become of him when I can no longer protect him. Silly fears of an old woman. No doubt Hannah felt the same for Samuel, and look how long a life he lived. And yet, how difficult it must have been for her to yield up her son to Eli. Can a mother's heart ever be at full peace? To bear a child is to know joy and worry. Is it also to bear sorrow?

Does the Messiah's mother have the same joy and worry? My heart cannot but reach out to her. Whether or not we ever meet, we are linked together. It would be such a blessing to know her and speak with her, to give mutual support. Who else can share the same supernatural experience? We are mothers like all other mothers and yet different from them all, though, even then, she is different from me. She is, after all, the mother of my Lord.

Zechariah

Now while he was serving as priest before God when his division was on duty, according to the custom of the priesthood, he was chosen by lot to enter the temple of the Lord and burn incense. And the whole multitude of the people were praying outside at the hour of incense. And there appeared to him an angel of the Lord standing on the right side of the altar of incense. And Zechariah was troubled when he saw him, and fear fell upon him.

—Luke 1:8–12

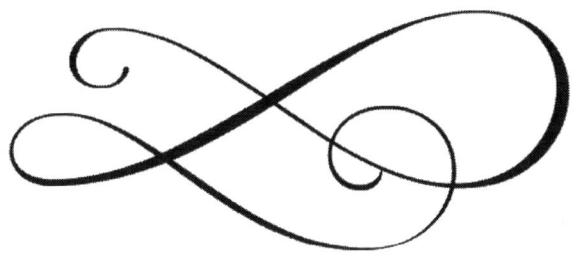

For full story:
Luke 1:5–23, 57–79

I know it was a foolish thing to say. Believe me, I know. I can't forget that day. Without an angel, it already had become the greatest day of my life. I had been chosen by lot to burn incense on the golden altar for that day's services. I had served more than forty years without the lot ever falling my way. And that's it. Once chosen, you are never given opportunity again. It is literally a once in a lifetime experience.

Forgive me then if I wasn't thinking straight. All my attention, all my energy was devoted to the task of placing the incense on the fire at the signal, which would then begin the day for sacrifices and worship. Such honor and responsibility—nothing was more momentous for me than this occasion.

Just after I laid the incense on the altar and the smoke was rising as a symbol of God receiving the sacrifices to be offered, at that moment the angel appeared next to the altar. I wasn't just startled; I was troubled; indeed, I was terrified. Had I done something wrong with the ritual? Was he going to slay me as Aaron's sons were immediately slain for making a wrong offering?

I just stood there, unable to move except for my uncontrollable trembling. Then what he said was the last thing, the very last thing I expected him to say—Elizabeth was going to have a baby. Where did that come from? What did that have to do with the moment?

A baby? He goes on about how much of a delight he will be to us. A baby? He will be great in the sight of the Lord and filled with the Holy Spirit. By the way, no wine or alcohol. Oh sure, what? A baby? He is to go in the spirit of Elijah and prepare the way for the Lord. Oh wow, that's something. Did you say a baby? How can I really know this? My wife and I are old.

I know it was a stupid thing to say. I wasn't thinking. Would you? You have a mighty angel appear out of nowhere in front of you while you are in the midst of the holiest act that you can do for your country, and then you keep your wits about you when he tells you that you and your barren wife will have a baby!

To be truthful with you, it wasn't just that Gabriel brought up an unexpected subject. You have to realize, we were childless. Do you know how I had longed to have a son? I like girls too, but a son to carry on my name—do you know what that means? After a while you learn to keep your emotions in check and not to get your hopes aroused. We had long resigned ourselves that a child was not in God's will for us. That's okay. We were not bitter. But…well…that's why I questioned Gabriel. I knew better, but he had touched a nerve and I couldn't help myself.

I suppose I got off easy being struck mute. My wife didn't take it too hard, especially after she became pregnant. With Mary's visit she had someone to talk with. When my son was born I expected to get my speech back. Gabriel had said that I would be mute until "these things" took place. I thought he meant my son's birth. What more needed to be done? Oh yes…his name. I got a chuckle out of everyone's perplexity when Elizabeth said he would be called John. When everyone inquired of me, I wrote, not his name will be or should be, but "His name *is* John." There was no naming to do. He already possessed the name that the Lord had given, which I should add, means "favored of Yahweh."

I did a lot of thinking during those months of Elizabeth's pregnancy. I thought about what Gabriel had said. He would be "great in the sight of the Lord." My son would be great, my son! He would turn back many to God; my son would do this! And he would be filled with the Holy Spirit like the prophets of old, even like the mightiest of them, Elijah. My son! My son—now get this—my son would prepare the way for the Lord. The prophecies of Isaiah were about to be fulfilled. The Messiah was coming! The words burst out of me when my son was born.

> Blessed be the Lord God of Israel,
>   for he has visited and redeemed his people
> and has raised up a horn of salvation for us
>   in the house of his servant David,

> as he spoke by the mouth of his holy prophets from of old,
> that we should be saved from our enemies
>   and from the hand of all who hate us;
> to show the mercy promised to our fathers
>   and to remember his holy covenant,
> the oath that he swore to our father Abraham, to grant us
>   that we, being delivered from the hand of our enemies,
> might serve him without fear,
>   in holiness and righteousness before him all our days.

Never has there been a father more proud than I, holding him in my arms and prophesying over him.

> And you, child, will be called the prophet of the Most High;
>   for you will go before the Lord to prepare his ways,
> to give knowledge of salvation to his people
>   in the forgiveness of their sins,
> because of the tender mercy of our God,
>   whereby the sunrise shall visit us from on high
> to give light to those who sit in darkness and in the shadow
>   of death,
>   to guide our feet into the way of peace.

"To give knowledge of salvation to his people in the forgiveness of their sins"—is that not a beautiful mission? My child will prepare the way of the Lord. My child will announce the coming of the Messiah.

Surely my son will be great in the eyes of God's people. He will go forth in the spirit and power of Elijah. My son, John, will turn the hearts of the fathers to the children, and the disobedient to the wisdom of the just. It is he who will make ready for the Lord a people prepared. What greater role can one play than this? Again, what did the angel say to me? Ah yes, I will have joy and gladness, and many will rejoice at my son's birth. For he will be great before the Lord. Many rejoice now and many more in the years to come when my son begins his calling.

I only pray that I will live to see John fulfill that calling. What joy that would be! But I am an old man. I do not know how many more days my God has numbered for me. Whatever time I do have, I must use it well to prepare my son for his work. I must teach him the sacred writings of the prophets who came before him, especially of Isaiah and Malachi who spoke of the messenger that my son is to be. Of Isaiah:

> A voice cries:
> "In the wilderness prepare the way of the Lord;
>   make straight in the desert a highway for our God.
> Every valley shall be lifted up,
>   and every mountain and hill be made low;
> the uneven ground shall become level,
>   and the rough places a plain.
> And the glory of the Lord shall be revealed,
>   and all flesh shall see it together,
>   for the mouth of the Lord has spoken."

Of Malachi:

> Behold, I will send you Elijah the prophet before the great and awesome day of the Lord comes. And he will turn the hearts of fathers to their children and the hearts of children to their fathers.

My heart is already turned to my child. May he be used to turn the hearts of us all to our God as he prepares the way for the Messiah. Prepare the way, John; prepare the way of the Lord.

The Shepherd

And in the same region there were shepherds out in the field, keeping watch over their flock by night. And an angel of the Lord appeared to them, and the glory of the Lord shone around them, and they were filled with great fear.

—Luke 2:8–9

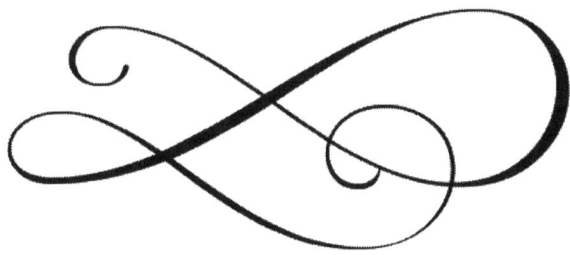

For full story:
Luke 2:8–20

I have never been so scared in my life. And I have had reasons to be frightened in my line of work. What, with long hours in the wilderness night protecting my flock, there have been enough times when a lion or a bear has attacked the sheep. I did my best to run them off, but I've neither the courage nor the strength of David who slew them by himself. It is one thing to see lions and bears at a distance. It is far different to be confronted by one and hear his growl. Your hairs stand on end, and it takes a brave heart to keep from shaking or running.

But nothing compares to this night of the angels appearing. First there was one angel. At least I wasn't alone. There are several of us. We are not far out in the wilderness. Our flock is a special one, selected to provide the temple sacrifices. Therefore, we are near Jerusalem, just outside Bethlehem, in fact. This is a safer environment for the sheep. We had them gathered in their pens. Some of the guys were about to settle for sleep while the others of us took the first shift of watch.

At that moment an angel appeared. I don't mean for that to sound common. I don't mean an angel appeared like, oh, a villager appeared. I mean *an angel!* How did I know it was an angel? It's not like I know a lot about angels, but when someone appears out of thin air with a light shining all about him, I figure it is an angel. But even more, it's hard to explain, but there's a feeling of being in the presence of holiness. Do you remember when God appeared to Moses in the burning bush and Moses fell on his face? All I can say is that I know how he felt. I was afraid before that angel, but it wasn't the kind of fear of facing a lion; somehow it was more frightening and yet wonderful at the same time. Is there such a thing as a holy fear?

The first thing the angel said was, "Fear not." Yeah, right; that put me at my ease. But then he continued, "For behold, I bring you good news of a great joy that will be for all the people." I must have begun to relax a bit, because, to tell you the truth, I don't think I've ever listened more attentively to anyone. We were about to hear a message from the Lord. I know what angels do. They deliver messages from God. And we were about to get one!

"For unto you is born this day in the city of David a Savior, who is Messiah the Lord." The Messiah! He's announcing the birth of the Messiah! This isn't just a message; it is *the* message that our people have waited to hear for centuries.

The angel goes on: "And this will be a sign for you: you will find a baby wrapped in swaddling cloths and lying in a manger." Well now, that is an odd sign; not exactly what one would expect of the Messiah. But that's okay; the point is the angel was telling us that we could go see him. The Messiah! Yes, us shepherds. I know it sounds crazy. Why tell us, and why should we be the privileged ones to go see him? I don't know, and I didn't ask.

I didn't have a chance to ask, because suddenly—and I mean suddenly—there's not one angel, but a multitude of angels—more than I could count—shouting out in praise to God. It was overwhelming. I fell flat on my face, but still I heard what they said clearly: "Glory to God in the highest, and on earth peace among those with whom he is pleased." I trembled all over again. My heart raced. My eyes—I could just open enough to catch a glimpse through the light.

And then they were gone. The angels vanished. The night was peaceful again as though nothing had happened. It was like waking from a dream, except the vision and the message remained clear. We decided to immediately find the baby. It didn't take too long in a small town, even with a lot of visitors, to find where a new baby had been born. And just as we were told, we found him wrapped in swaddling cloths, lying in a manger.

We fell on our knees before him. We didn't stay long. We told the parents what had happened and after a while slipped out. But I tell you, we were so happy we could have burst. We went out shouting praise to God. People asked us what we were so happy about. We told them about the child and what the angel had said. They were amazed, but they also thought we were drunk or fools.

You've got to wonder why we were given the message in the first place. We are but poor shepherds. Most of our time is spent in the wilderness outside the cities and towns. We certainly have no religious status or authority. Why should anyone listen to us?

Isn't it strange how God chooses the foolish to show his wisdom? We may be fools, but I will tell you this—we are at least fools willing to listen. We are not educated scribes who know how to debate, but we do know how to listen and to obey and to believe. I'll be truthful with you; the Messiah looked like an ordinary baby. Even so, I believe and I am happy this night.

The Good Shepherd has not forgotten his flock, Israel. He has sent another Shepherd-King like David. However poor and humble my position may be, it, nevertheless, is a proud heritage. Our father Abraham was a shepherd, as were Isaac and Jacob, as were all my people in the land of Egypt. And, of course, there was David. My father taught me that it would be from his line that the Messiah would come, and like David, he would shepherd Israel like a flock and guide them with a skillful hand. I, too, should then faithfully watch over my flock.

I am not surprised to find that the Messiah begins his life in such a humble manner. That may not be fitting for a promised king, but it is for a promised shepherd. He may begin in humility, but no doubt he will rise to great heights of glory. But however great a king he will become, I've no doubt that he will remain in his spirit a shepherd.

I know my sheep by name. I can call each of them, and each will come to me because he recognizes the voice of his shepherd. They feel secure when I am around. Likewise, the time will come soon, once this baby grows to be a man, that we will all hear the voice of our Shepherd call us to himself, our Shepherd-Savior. He will bring us deliverance. He will bring us peace.

I feel like my life has changed, even though I have gone back to my flock. In a few days priests will come and select lambs to be offered at the temple. All the more diligent I must be in my care of them, for only the unblemished can be chosen for the sacrifices. Only the blood from a sheep without blemish can be used to atone for sin. Perhaps someday the Messiah will himself choose a lamb from my flock when he makes his sacrifice. Glory to God in the highest!

Mary

And Mary said,

"My soul magnifies the Lord,
   and my spirit rejoices in God my Savior,
for he has looked on the humble estate of his servant.
   For behold, from now on all generations will call me blessed;
for he who is mighty has done great things for me,
   and holy is his name."

—Luke 1:46–49

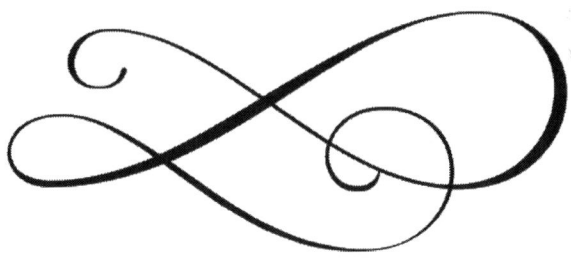

For full story:
Luke 1:26–56

The night is finally quiet. The shepherds have left. My husband and my baby are fast asleep.

Joseph was so tired. The year has been emotionally exhausting for him. He thought he had found in me a woman with whom to share a peaceful life, despite the hard work we had as a peasant couple. Labor is not a burden. Shame is a heavy weight to bear. He felt the shame hardest when I first told him the news of my pregnancy. I did not expect him to believe my story. He was ashamed of me—me, whom he loved and even respected for my reverence of God. I could see the despair in his face. He would be assumed the father. He could have taken me before the elders and cleared his name, yet he was not that kind of man. He had to divorce me, to be sure, but he would do so quietly.

Then he too is visited by an angel of the Lord. He no longer doubts me, and, like me, is obedient. He takes me as his wife. And yet, that did not erase the talk. Clearly, I was already pregnant. My husband must live with the shame of being thought by his townspeople that he had shamed me. We could tell no one of the angelic visits. Who would believe? The stories would have only invited ridicule.

Then came the ten-day trip to Bethlehem. Joseph was responsible for me and he felt the burden of that responsibility. That I bore the Son of God, the promised Messiah, made him worry all the more. He tried to hide it, but I am his wife. I could see the anxiety. And yet my husband brought me safely here and my child is born. All has happened according to the plan of the Lord, as I knew it would be.

I did not know how the will of the Lord would play out, only that I would bear miraculously the Messiah, the holy Son of God. The angel did not tell me that I would have a husband, only that I would have a child.

I had to clarify how I would conceive. I hoped that Joseph would still have me, but I had no reason to believe he would. I knew nothing of my future other than bearing God's holy child.

But then, that was enough for me. The Lord God owed me no explanation; I owed him obedience. The choice to do his will was not complicated. I am his servant; I need only to know his will. And whatever he calls on me to do, he will provide the means to carry it out.

Then came the further confirmations. The visit to my cousin Elizabeth, also pregnant, and one well past the childbearing age.

"Blessed are you among women, and blessed is the fruit of your womb! And why is this granted to me that the mother of my Lord should come to me? For behold, when the sound of your greeting came to my ears, the baby in my womb leaped for joy. And blessed is she who believed that there would be a fulfillment of what was spoken to her from the Lord."

Truly I did feel blessed and still do. Truly I had believed the fulfillment of the angel's message, and all the more do I believe that what has been spoken of my baby will come true.

How it will all take place, I do not know, only that God's word will be fulfilled. And so, as I responded to Elizabeth, I say again, "My soul magnifies the Lord, and my spirit rejoices in God my Savior." For, as the mother of the Son of the Most High, I truly will be called blessed by generations to come. I do not know why I was chosen, only that the Lord delights in lifting up those of humble estate. Oh, truly I am blessed! My child the Messiah. My child the holy Son of the Most High!

Then Joseph told me of the angel's visit to him in a dream. This son will save his people from their sins. That is the reason for his name Jesus—God saves. All the pieces were coming together: the confirmations, Joseph taking me in marriage, even the trip to Bethlehem where we could start over again. The Lord is faithful.

And this very night I deliver. Already I am filled with awe and joy when shepherds, of all people, come to the house seeking the baby. They tell us of their angelic visit, of the news that a Savior who is the Messiah, who is the Lord has been born; that they would find him even in this manger. They tell of how the sky was filled with angels giving praise and glory to God. What a wondrous sight that must have been. The shepherds' faces were certainly filled with wonder. And then they left shouting out their own doxology to God.

And now, finally, there is quiet and peace. What next? I know not what tomorrow brings, much less the coming years. God's kingdom has drawn nigh, this I know. The promise of the kingdom, the promise first made to our father Abraham in making him a blessing to many nations is soon to be fulfilled in my child, in the Lord's son, the Messiah. This child sleeping so peacefully will bring peace to our people.

I have thought of the angel's words about him. My son will be great and will be called the Son of the Most High. And the Lord God will give to him the throne of his father David, and he will reign over the house of Jacob forever, and of his kingdom there will be no end. The Son of the Most High. His father is no less than God himself. How can this be? Does that mean that my son also is divine? How else is his kingdom to be without end? Is such a thought blasphemy?

This child is my own flesh and blood. I carried him in my womb and gave him birth. I hold him now in my arms. This child so close, so much of me, and yet, who is he really? Can I even say that he is mine? There is so much to ponder.

What will come before the throne? Will Herod accept him? Will the Romans give away their rule without a fight? Is my child to be a great warrior? Are there battles for him to fight? Surely he is to be a great king. I have still much to learn. But learn, I shall, and all in God's good time.

I already know what is needed from me. I am to mother my child. Love him, nurture him, protect him. For now, he is but a baby. He needs only now my milk to nourish him, my arms to secure him. He needs his mother.

What will take place next will take place under the Lord's sovereign plan. I am but his servant. Let the future be according to his word. Let my son Jesus become the Messiah who delivers his people even from their sin and their bondage. Whatever should happen to me before then, let it be in my son's service and to the glory of God. May I be a good mother to my son, a faithful servant to my Lord. If so, then I am at peace, and truly I will be blessed.

> My soul magnifies the Lord,
>   and my spirit rejoices in God my Savior,
> for he has looked on the humble estate of his servant.
>   For behold, from now on all generations will call me blessed.

I am blessed now, indeed.

Anna

And there was a prophetess, Anna, the daughter of Phanuel, of the tribe of Asher. She was advanced in years, having lived with her husband seven years from when she was a virgin, and then as a widow until she was eighty-four. She did not depart from the temple, worshiping with fasting and prayer night and day. And coming up at that very hour she began to give thanks to God and to speak of him to all who were waiting for the redemption of Jerusalem.

—Luke 2:36–38

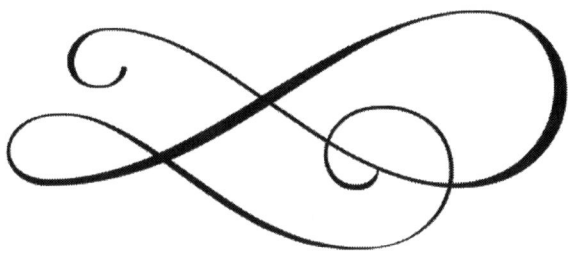

For full story:
Luke 2:22–38

I suppose my life has been unusual. I possibly could have remarried after my husband died. We had been married but seven years. I was still young enough to be considered a desirable wife except that I had born no children. Seven years, no child—a man would have taken a risk with me. But then, I did not desire remarriage. My father had made the arrangements for the first. My husband treated me well enough. Even so, after his death I had no yearning to be a wife again. I had always been content to be known as the daughter of Phanuel, and so, that is how I continued my life.

But if not remarriage, then what? I could have returned home to my father's house. He and my brothers would have seen that I was provided for. I could have returned, if not for my calling as a prophetess. A prophetess can live anywhere, but the Lord called me to serve him in Jerusalem, in the temple courts. There are rooms on the grounds for the priests who serve their rotations and who take care of the temple and preparations. They have allowed me a small room, perhaps out of recognition of my calling, perhaps out of kindness for a widow.

Whatever they may think of my calling, they have come to respect my constancy. Year after year, decade after decade I have worshiped, fasted, and prayed in the temple, and yes, I have prophesied. You might even say I have enacted the prophecy I was given.

Why the temple? What prophet carried out his or her entire ministry in the temple as I have? Night and day I have remained on this holy ground, doing what everyone else makes temporary trips to do—to offer up to God his due worship and to lift up prayers of supplication. For those with ears to hear—better yet, with eyes to see—my very actions have been my prophecy. I am not like the first prophetess, Miriam, who prophesied in song and with tambourine. I am not like Deborah who judged over the tribes of Israel. Nor am I like Huldah with whom royal officials consulted. I am the prophetess who has worshiped night and day in the temple.

I have done so for a reason. It is my calling to prophesy before Israel to remember her true King and to trust in the coming of the Messiah, who will restore the throne of David. In that day, Israel will find her true and lasting redemption.

Too easily my people look to man, and to woman, for their redemption. They place their hope in intrigues, in political maneuvers, placing their bets on who will win the next political struggle. Will Herod keep his throne? What is his son Antipater up to now? Will he or another son succeed? As if it mattered. I have lived long on this temple mount, far earlier than when Herod began his reign thirty years ago. I remember when Judea was free, ruled by our own people from the line of the Maccabees and Hasmoneans. Were those not the glorious years? The king and the high priest were the same. And yet, even then the corruption of power seeped in, and our rulers and would-be rulers fell to the same intrigues and battles going on today. The best ruler was a woman—Alexandria. My father told me that she had the most common sense. Her sons fought for control. Hyrcanus won out, but he was really a puppet of another ruler. It gets complicated. The Romans finally came in, and Herod sits on the throne as a seemingly powerful king, but one who can be deposed whenever the Roman emperor gives the word.

Hear the words of the psalmist:

> It is better to take refuge in the LORD
>   than to trust in man.
> It is better to take refuge in the LORD
>   than to trust in princes.

I worship at the temple as prophecy that I acknowledge and worship the true King over all, who sits on his throne in the Most Holy Place. Do not mistake me. I understand that the Lord sits in his throne in heaven, but it is here, in the temple, in the Most Holy Place that he has called his people to worship him as their only rightful King. I remain on these temple grounds to remind our people not to lose sight of who reigns over us and over all kings and princes.

I have prayed in the temple courts night and day, not because I am especially godly, but because I am displaying to our people whom we are to place our hope in. We have spent too much effort petitioning the latest king or governor or emperor for what we want. We think that a man or a woman with a title, or with connections to the right person with a title, will get us justice or the favor we desire. We gather around the palace or the houses of officials, thinking that it is in those places where the power lies. We have forgotten where the real power lies—here in the temple where sits the Lord of Hosts. My actions form the testimony that there are those of us who have not forgotten the hope of the Messiah who will bring the redemption of the Lord.

And now, praise be the Lord Who Provides, for after eighty years I can prophesy that the Messiah, our Redeemer has come! Come in a way that I had not even foreseen. I knew that it would be in the temple that the Lord's redemption would appear. But as a child? As an infant? To a poor father? And yet, so the psalmist prophesied:

> The stone that the builders rejected
> has become the cornerstone.

The father, and even the mother, attest that they come from the lineage of David, the tribe of Judah. Therefore, at the right time, he will return to Jerusalem and take up the throne that belongs to the house of David. Some day he will return, and as the Maccabean rulers had tried to do, he will truly accomplish, for he will be both King and High Priest. He will be the Prophet that Moses prophesied would come. He will be the Messiah, the Anointed One. He will be our Redeemer. He will be the Cornerstone.

> This is the Lord's doing;
>   it is marvelous in our eyes.
> This is the day that the Lord has made;
>   let us rejoice and be glad in it.

Then will be the true redemption of Jerusalem, God's city.

> Jerusalem—built as a city
>   that is bound firmly together,
> to which the tribes go up,
>   the tribes of the Lord,
> as was decreed for Israel,
>   to give thanks to the name of the Lord.
> There thrones for judgment were set,
>   the thrones of the house of David.

The throne of the house of David shall be established once again and then forever in this city of Jerusalem. To Jerusalem not only will the tribes of Israel come but all nations with their kings. Then shall the prophecy of Isaiah be fulfilled.

> For Zion's sake I will not keep silent,
>   and for Jerusalem's sake I will not be quiet,
> until her righteousness goes forth as brightness,
>   and her salvation as a burning torch.
> The nations shall see your righteousness,
>   and all the kings your glory,
> and you shall be called by a new name
>   that the mouth of the Lord will give.
> You shall be a crown of beauty in the hand of the Lord,
>   and a royal diadem in the hand of your God.
> You shall no more be termed Forsaken,
>   and your land shall no more be termed Desolate,
> but you shall be called My Delight Is in Her,
>   and your land Married;
> for the Lord delights in you,
>   and your land shall be married.
> For as a young man marries a young woman,
>   so shall your sons marry you,
> and as the bridegroom rejoices over the bride,
>   so shall your God rejoice over you.
> Go through, go through the gates;
>   prepare the way for the people;
> build up, build up the highway;
>   clear it of stones;

> lift up a signal over the peoples.
> Behold, the LORD has proclaimed
>   to the end of the earth:
> Say to the daughter of Zion,
>   "Behold, your salvation comes;
> behold, his reward is with him,
>   and his recompense before him."
> And they shall be called The Holy People,
>   The Redeemed of the LORD;
> and you shall be called Sought Out,
>   A City Not Forsaken.

Praise be to the Lord of Hosts, who sits upon his heavenly throne, that he has heard my prayers, and the prayers of all his people who have loyally kept hope for the redemption of Jerusalem. To all who will hear, behold, your salvation comes. Your King is coming to you!

The Wise Man

Now after Jesus was born in Bethlehem of Judea in the days of Herod the king, behold, wise men from the east came to Jerusalem, saying, "Where is he who has been born king of the Jews?"

—Matthew 2:1–2

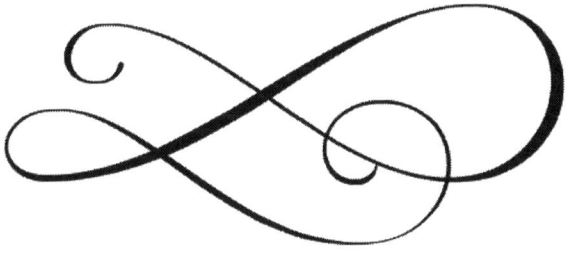

For full story:
Matthew 2:1–12

From the east. Yes, we had traveled from the east. That is enough to know, enough for us to reveal. To leave our land was already difficult without word returning home that we had left to pay homage to a new king. It was a risky venture to leave, then to travel through dangerous lands, and, as we came to learn, to arrive in the most hostile land of all.

Wise men? Is that what we were? We are considered so in our own land, enough so to serve as counselors to rulers. Much wisdom is needed to keep our heads as counselors to kings who are ever suspicious in their insecurity. But the truly wise understand how little wisdom anyone has. One needs only to look up to the stars to grasp the insignificance of our so-called wisdom and knowledge.

And yet it is to the stars that we look for knowledge and understanding. It is in the heavens where the wonder dwells.

> When I look at your heavens, the work of your fingers,
>   the moon and the stars, which you have set in place,
> what is man that you are mindful of him,
>   and the son of man that you care for him?

Surprised that we should know these words of Israel's King David? We know others. Here is from the prophet Isaiah.

> Lift up your eyes on high and see:
>   who created these?
> He who brings out their host by number,
>   calling them all by name,
> by the greatness of his might,
>   and because he is strong in power
>   not one is missing.

Do not be surprised. Are we not wise men, seekers of knowledge? Yes, we look at the stars; we also search the ancient writings of many countries, including the land of ancient Israel. Where we live there is a colony of the Jews and their rabbis. And knowledge seekers of every land will search and share knowledge with other seekers.

A few of us became interested in the sacred writings of the Jews. They worship one God. We too had come to such a view even in the midst of our polytheist society. Their religion is ancient and yet far advanced those of their surrounding cultures. Where other religions seem to grope for answers, theirs possess revelation from the one God.

Is it revelation? We were open to it. The story of the one Creator who creates all the world and the universe and then makes man in his image—that rings true to us, as does the story of the fall. How else to account for both the wisdom and folly of man, for his majestic achievements and his barbarous cruelty? How much more glorious is the Yahweh God in his holiness than the petty, vacillating gods and goddesses of the nations and tribes. Even the sacrifices and cultic practices of Yahweh have greater sense of purpose and dignity.

We conversed much with the Jewish rabbis, seeking to understand fully their religion. For a downtrodden people whose history is filled with defeats and eventual exile, they remain ever hopeful that their Yahweh God will restore their fortunes. They refer to the kingdom of God that will someday be restored; no, rather a kingdom that will be consummated with the coming of the Great King, the Anointed One.

It may seem a silly idea, but then again, our hearts were stirred. We inquired more. This king is the king of the Jews, true, but through them he is to become the king of us all. He will not be against us; he will belong to us or, rather, we to him—all of us from every nation and tribe and tongues. It is there in their sacred scriptures. The blessing given to their father Abraham was to flow through him to all the nations. The people of Israel were to be a nation of priests leading the rest of us to their Yahweh God. And then there was to come the Servant, the Anointed One, who was to be light even to the Gentiles, who was to establish a kingdom to which all the nations would come in peace and receive justice. A king for all of us, just as there is one God over us all! This is a king worth believing in, an idea to devote ourselves to understanding.

And then the star appeared! Now we were in the area of knowledge we knew best. Do not scoff at us so quickly. We are not fortune tellers and base astrologers who believe that the stars control our destinies. But cannot God use whatever signs he so deems to communicate by, especially to those of us outside the chosen people?

> The heavens declare the glory of God,
>   and the sky above proclaims his handiwork.
> Day to day pours out speech,
>   and night to night reveals knowledge.

We believe the star signaled that what the sacred writings spoke of has indeed come true—the Anointed King, the Messiah, has been born!

And so we traveled from out of the east to seek the one born king of the Jews who would become king of the world. We traveled to behold the king and to pay him homage. We could not speak of it in our homeland, and we came to learn that we should not have spoken of it in his homeland.

Of course we traveled to Jerusalem, the capital of Israel. Where else should he be? We did not know exactly what to expect, but we thought that surely his birth would be known by his own people. Surely the religious teachers could tell us something. And yet, our questions only raised fears. It was not long before we were summoned before King Herod.

He had heard about our quest. He also was eager to pay homage to this new king. He must be the Messiah. The Jews had been looking for his coming, especially he had. He considered himself but a steward ready to turn over the kingdom to the Messiah. How surprising that he had heard no word about the child's birth. When had we seen the star? He had already consulted with the chief learned men, and they said that Bethlehem should have been the birthplace. Would we go there, and bring him word when we found him, that he too might come and worship him? He would go with us except that his presence might cause undue consternation among the people. Evidently whoever had care for the child had thought it not time for the king's birth to be made public. Understandable considering the hostility of the Romans, he noted.

He had us leave quietly in the night. No public scene. We were glad to leave. We have enough experience with kings to discern their connivances. Even without the dream that warned us about Herod, we had no intention of returning to him.

We were not far from Bethlehem when we saw the star, this time not from afar but near and low to the earth, so low that we could follow to the very spot it shone over. Great joy filled our hearts as we came to the house of the king—a small, plain dwelling. The father opened the door and before us was the mother with the child sitting on her lap. We no sooner entered than we fell to our knees and bowed before him. We presented our gifts, and then we left even that very night after the dream came.

We have returned home. We have told no one the truth of whom we traveled to see. Perhaps when the time comes for his revealing, but then we are already old. Will we still be alive? Why then did we go, if it were not for the purpose of spreading the news? Why seek knowledge if we will not share it?

It was not for the sake of knowledge that we traveled to a distant land. It was for the sake of worship, to pay homage to our king. We are of a people who walk in darkness, and we have seen a great light. The light is the light of the world. You might say that we came as representatives of the world. Let it be known whenever the Messiah's time is revealed that men came "from the east" to worship the king of all people of all nations.

> Arise, shine, for your light has come,
>   and the glory of the Lord has risen upon you.
> For behold, darkness shall cover the earth,
>   and thick darkness the peoples;
> but the Lord will arise upon you,
>   and his glory will be seen upon you.
> And nations shall come to your light,
>   and kings to the brightness of your rising.

Joseph

Now the birth of Jesus Christ took place in this way. When his mother Mary had been betrothed to Joseph, before they came together she was found to be with child from the Holy Spirit. And her husband Joseph, being a just man and unwilling to put her to shame, resolved to divorce her quietly. But as he considered these things, behold, an angel of the Lord appeared to him in a dream.

—Matthew 1:18–20

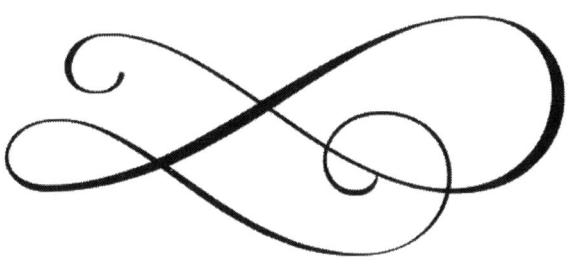

For full story:
Matthew 1:18–2:15, 19–23; Luke 2:41–51

Given my name, I suppose it is fitting that I should be given dreams from the Lord. I did not grow up having such dreams. Certainly no one ever said of me, "Here comes the dreamer." I am a carpenter in keeping with my father's trade. I work hard. I am no daydreamer. I follow as faithfully as I know the law and fear the Holy One. I try to do what is right.

My parents arranged my betrothal with Mary, and I was well pleased. Mary was a young maiden who also worked hard with her family. She did not flirt but was modest, and, as beautiful as I thought she was, it was her inner beauty that radiated. Mary too followed the law and feared God, but her obedience seemed to come naturally. I disciplined myself to be obedient; she needed no such discipline.

All the more then that her pregnancy was so shocking. The sin itself is shameful enough. We live in a small village. We live in a village where the women remain chaste until marriage, and no one would even be tempted to commit adultery with a man who is not her betrothed. If Mary had claimed that a man had forced himself upon her, but no, she claimed that she had remained chaste. Any explanation would have been better than what she came up with—the Holy Spirit? the power of the Most High? the Son of God? Was she also willing to commit blasphemy? Was she demon possessed? What had happened to my Mary?

I could not go through with the marriage, of course. But then, neither could I publicly disgrace her. The very nature of the sin did not square with what I knew of her, and she stood her ground with her explanation. She was not a liar, and her ongoing demeanor belied the notion of demon possession. And so I resolved to quietly end the betrothal. Perhaps she could return to her cousin Elizabeth and escape the disgrace that would befall her in Nazareth.

Then the first dream came. The angel, just as Mary had described him, came to me. Mary had been truthful all along. The conception had come from the Holy Spirit. I was to marry her and take care of her and the child Jesus, the son who was God's Son. I was both relieved and fearful. I did not fear the villagers. I could bear reproach, and gladly bear it with my wife. It was the responsibility that unnerved me. Could I protect God's son from disgrace?

The Roman decree that forced us to travel to Bethlehem actually came at a good time. It was a difficult journey to make, but it also took us out of our small village and the disgrace that came with living there. We would be fine in my hometown. I had family and could find work. But the weight of responsibility grew heavier from the moment the child was born. Every father feels the weight when the first child is born: "I now have a child to provide for." Imagine the realization, "I have God's son to provide for."

The very evening of his birth, we met the first of astonishing characters. Shepherds came. They had been visited by an angel who announced the birth of the Messiah who is to be Savior. And here they were right where the angel had directed them. Forty days later we took the child to the temple in Jerusalem for Mary's purification and to consecrate the child. There we were met by an old man named Simeon who proclaimed him to be the Messiah, the light for Gentiles that Isaiah had spoken of. Immediately after Simeon came an old woman named Anna who also spoke of him as the Redeemer. How am I to provide for him?

Things settled down. We remained in Bethlehem, where I expected us to stay the rest of our lives. I knew nothing else to do other than continue as a carpenter. Two years later came the most astonishing characters of all—Gentiles, and not just Gentiles but magi who were obviously wealthy. They came, they said, to worship the king of the Jews, and then they bowed down before the boy and offered very costly gifts.

I had no doubt even before this episode that the child had come from God and was the Messiah that we Jews had awaited for centuries. But is his kingship to extend over the Gentiles? Where do we fit in? Why had Mary and I been chosen for his parents? We were poor. And how is all this to take place? How was this child to one day rise up as Israel's deliverer? Did I need somehow to help make this happen? What was I to do?

I was soon to find out. The visit of the magi brought not only treasure but danger. I was visited a second time in a dream by an angel, warning me to flee to Egypt with the child and Mary. Herod was now aware of his existence and would seek his death. I had to protect Jesus. The gifts proved a godsend, as they provided the means to pay for our journey and years in Egypt. I protected my child in a foreign land and brought him back safely to our original home in Nazareth after two more dreams directed me. Herod had died, but his son Archelaus was reigning over Judah. It was safer to go back up into Galilee.

I would continue to protect my son, though it was in the strangest of places that I feared I had failed. As the law directs, we attended the Feast of the Passover every year in Jerusalem. When my son, Jesus, was twelve (one year before the age of manhood) we lost him. We left the city in a large group of family and fellow villagers, thinking that he was with relatives. He had always been an obedient boy. We never had to worry about him. But he did not show up when we camped. He was gone! No one knew where. We had left him alone in Jerusalem!

Imagine how frantic we were, and our worries only grew. Though we searched and searched, we could not find him, not until the third day in the temple courts. As we walked along the colonnade where rabbis taught their disciples, we heard our son's voice. The rabbis were gathered around him, listening to him!

We both stood gaping. Mary reacted first. "Son, what do you think you are doing? Your father and I have been sick with worry about you. We have been searching for days for you!" He looked at us puzzled, "Wouldn't you know that I would be here in my Father's house? Where else would I be?"

I knew my role and had accepted it obediently, even gladly, however fearful the responsibility might be. Yes, I was to be the protector and provider for God's Son. Even so, as he grew under my watch, I had come to see him as my son, my beloved son. I had almost forgotten his true Father, who was his true Protector and Provider. My...his Son had never forgotten his Father. There was a relationship between that Father and Son that was growing stronger by the year, and this year before his age of manhood the Son would make it clear who the Father was that he owed his allegiance.

Somehow the thought did not sadden me. It brought me back to a day in which I held a baby in my arms and pronounced his name Jesus. I dreamed then of what he would become, how he would be the Messiah who would save his people from their sins. And here he was, in his Father's house, exhibiting his Father's wisdom. The son of the carpenter was in truth the Son of God. How could I not be proud of my son who would fulfill the dreams of all who looked for their Redeemer and so become children of his Father?

PART TWO

And Dwelt Among Us

The Angel in the Wilderness

Then Jesus was led up by the Spirit into the wilderness to be tempted by the devil. And after fasting forty days and forty nights, he was hungry. And the tempter came …

—Matthew 4:1–3

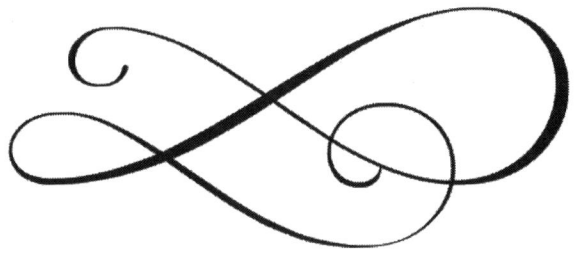

For full story:
Matthew 4:1–11

We were given orders to safeguard Jesus during his time in the wilderness. Keep wild animals from harming him—like a lion or bear or snake. Snake! If only we were allowed to protect him from that Serpent bent on leading him astray, just as he led the first Adam. None of us angels will ever forget that dreadful day.

We marveled at God's new creation—such wondrous mountains and seas and forests, such amazing creatures large and small and of every color, shape, and size. But nothing matched the man and woman made in his image. In his image! We could not wait to see how they would govern this new world. With all of their intellectual faculties joined with their Creator's holiness and love, the future seemed ripe with all kinds of possibilities for their race. We wondered what interactions we angels would get to have with them.

We forgot to take into account the Fallen Angel. How did he get into Paradise? But there he was tempting Eve and through her corrupting Adam. And all we were allowed to do was watch, just as we are doing now over the second Adam.

This Adam is different, for though he is man he is also God—God the Son, to be precise. Here is someone even more wondrous than the first Adam, for he is not a new creature but the eternal God. Even we angels are baffled by the Trinity, but more baffling by the concept of Three Persons in One is the decision for the Second Person to become man. It is not like they are lonely. I must say that, besides the intimate relations of the Trinity, God does have us angels. Why send anyone, much less the Son of God, to save a rebellious race?

Yes, Satan deceived Adam and Eve, but they seemed rather willing to be deceived. They did not give up much of a fight. Think about it. They were living in Eden—in Paradise! They had everything they wanted, or I should say needed. And what lay before them? Glory upon glory. Joy upon joy. Eternal life lay before them, an eternal life filled with fruitfulness as they gave birth to a new race and as they discovered and invented and produced their own creations in imitation of their Creator. And still they fell! Oh, they were sorry afterwards, to be sure, especially as they learned of the punishments. But the Fall had happened, and misery and death entered into this beautiful world.

That is where it could have stayed if not for the mercy of the Creator, who even as he punished, he provided for them in their misery, and even… even at that moment spoke of a hope to come who would crush the Serpent's head. Now here is Hope in the form of man, and here is the Serpent awaiting him. We could do nothing but watch.

My first thought is "why the wilderness?" Adam was given a garden to meet his tempter. Jesus was led by the Third Person of the Trinity, the Holy Spirit, into the wilderness for his confrontation with the Enemy. And he is there for forty days (like the Israelites in the wilderness for forty years, now that I think about it). He is there for forty days without food! I sort of understand fasting (not really), but people fast to prepare for battle, not while fighting the battle. One might think that Satan only tempted Jesus three times. He was tempting Jesus for forty days.

I suppose Satan knew the wilderness experience was coming to an end. He struck literally for the gut with the challenge to turn stone into bread. As a man Jesus felt hunger pains. Forty days without food while living in the wilderness and wrestling against Satan—he would have been hungry enough. Actually I would have liked to see him do it. That would have shown Satan what he could do. But he held back. He replied with Scripture: "It is written, 'Man shall not live by bread alone.'" Maybe the fasting was connected with trusting his Father to provide?

Satan took a cue from that reply. He took Jesus to the top of the temple in Jerusalem and said to him, "If you are the Son of God, throw yourself down from here, for it is written,

>"'He will command his angels concerning you, to guard you,'

and

>"'On their hands they will bear you up,
>   lest you strike your foot against a stone.'"

"Yes, yes we will!" I thought. "I am ready!" My fellow angels and I nodded to one another. Perhaps this was why we were sent to watch over the situation.

But Jesus again declined. "Again it is written, 'You shall not put the Lord your God to the test.'" I had not thought about it that way. It seemed that trusting his Father was again the issue—not trusting the Father to send us but trusting the Father to know what is best for him. Jumping off temples was not in the plan for him. What is the plan?

Then came the final temptation. The Enemy took Jesus to a mountaintop and displayed the kingdoms of the world to him. With a flourish of his hand he proclaimed: "To you I will give all this authority and their glory, for it has been delivered to me, and I give it to whom I will. If you, then, will worship me, it will all be yours."

What a strange temptation. Worship Satan? It is Satan who should worship the Lord who stands before him! And what authority does the Rebel think he possesses? I expected Jesus to laugh. Instead, he seemed to take this offer most seriously of all.

"Be gone, Satan! For it is written,

>"'You shall worship the Lord your God
>   and him only shall you serve.'"

I was pleased to see Jesus finally get angry. But why now? What stirred up the emotions? Ah, yes; no doubt, he was remembering that first rebellion. Lucifer, we had called him: "Bringer of Light," the "Morning Star." Our Lord quoted Scripture in his reply, but these are words he had pronounced ages before the world was created. They were the words pronounced as the Morning Star was cast out of heaven. Would Satan never learn?

There will be no repeat of what took place when Satan succeeded in Adam being cast out of Eden. There will be no fall. A better Adam has appeared on the scene, and he is more than equal to the task. Satan has left, for now. No doubt he will return, but he has lost the first round, as he will no matter how often he comes and with whatever temptation he imagines. We unfallen angels chose the right champion.

Still, what is the anguish that my Lord wears upon his face? He has proven his strength, proven himself as Victor. He has come to save this human race of which he has now made himself the head. I know that he has come to restore what fell under the first Adam. That is his mission. And yet, now that he has won the first encounter against the Enemy, it seems that he expects a more terrible battle to come.

I remain as baffled as ever over the Son's mission. He gives up his equality with the Father to take on flesh, to become lower in that flesh than we angels to do what? He has battled Satan and won. Does he not now take control over the earth? I was with him when he overthrew Satan and cast him out of heaven? Why does he not now cast Satan from the earth? What more must be done?

Orders have arrived. We must go minister to him. He is weary and hungry.

The Servant at the Wedding in Cana

On the third day there was a wedding at Cana in Galilee, and the mother of Jesus was there. Jesus also was invited to the wedding with his disciples. When the wine ran out, the mother of Jesus said to him, "They have no wine." And Jesus said to her, "Woman, what does this have to do with me? My hour has not yet come." His mother said to the servants, "Do whatever he tells you."

—John 2:1–5

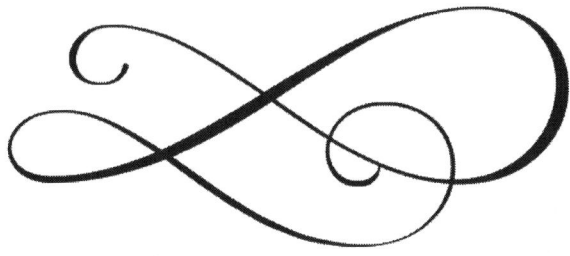

For full story:
John 2:1–11

Let me say first that I was not in charge of purchasing the wine. For months, the family had been planning for the banquet. They had all of us working nonstop to prepare the house, purchase supplies, do anything and everything to assure that everything was provided for. Purchasing was the responsibility of the steward. I had my doubts all along that he had bought enough. But then, I am just a servant. I do what I am told.

My assignment for the banquet was to serve the food and wine.

"Keep the wine cups filled, Benjamin," the master of the feast instructed me. "We want the guests merry."

It took several of us to keep up with the demand. And we were glad to serve. We love the son of our master, and we wanted his day of marriage to be joyous. That is how the banquet of the bridegroom and his bride ought to be. We certainly did not want anyone looking down on him and my master and mistress because they could not provide a rich feast. Generosity is what befits a noble family.

But I had my doubts when I first saw the amount of wine purchased. "Mark my words," I told Joel. "We are going to run out." And so we did.

Fortunately for my master, I kept my wits. It was useless to go to the steward. He would just get angry with me. I could not embarrass my master by appealing to his son's friend, the master of the feast. I certainly could not speak to the bridegroom or my master, who would be distressed, and ruin their joy.

Who then to turn to? You will think it strange, but I approached a female guest, Mary of Nazareth. She was a long-time friend of the family. Whenever she visited the house, she would graciously speak to me. I observed, over time, her bearing—her wisdom, how acutely observant she was. I knew she was a confidant for my mistress. And so, I knew she could be trusted, though, what she could actually do, I did not know. Maybe she could somehow advise me what to do.

What she did do embarrassed me. She turned to her son next to her and blurted out my dilemma. "They have no wine."

"Woman, what does this have to do with me? My hour has not yet come."

Okay, this was not going well. Did he just call his mother, woman? He looked peeved. Worse yet, his friends overheard. They all looked at the two and then at me. The last thing I needed was a scene between mother and son.

But all she did was turn to me and Joel, and said, "Do whatever he tells you."

The son's name was Jesus. I had seen most of Mary's children on her visits, but not him. I had heard rumors about him being a preacher of some sort. He was invited on his mother's account, though I don't recall his friends being on the list. That did not help with the wine supply, but I wasn't going to say anything.

I couldn't tell if Jesus was going to say anything to me. He was quiet. I could tell he was debating in his mind what to do. What could he do? Did he know a good source where we could get wine?

"Fill the jars with water."

We had six large stone water jars placed around the courtyard for washing our guests' hands. My master and his family were observant of the law. They kept themselves ceremonially clean, and they were careful to provide enough jars for their guests. We had borrowed four from neighbors. They held about thirty gallons. Of course, we did not need to fill the jars with that much water. About three-quarters full was more than enough.

Fill the jars with water? What did the jars of water have to do with anything? Why fill them? We didn't need more water. We needed more wine! But then, I am just a servant. I do what I am told, and I did not want to show disrespect to Mary.

So, Joel and I quietly, with a couple of the other servants, hurried to the house well, carried water over to the jars and filled them. It wasn't easy as we had to be secretive to keep the family and the master of the feast unaware.

We all felt foolish and that we were wasting our time. But we completed the job. Joel and I reported back to Jesus.

"Now draw some out and take it to the master of the feast."

Joel and I looked at each other. We sighed. Well, we are nothing but servants. We do what we are told. We took a ladle, drew out water, then handed it to another servant to give to the master of the feast. Then we watched.

He took a sip, and then another. His eyes gleamed. He walked over to the bridegroom. We followed.

"Everyone serves the good wine first, and when people have drunk freely, then the poor wine. But you have kept the good wine until now."

We ran back to the jar and drew our own cups. It was wine! We drew from every jar. It was all wine! Every jar filled to the brim! And the master of the feast was right. It was good wine. It was the best wine I had ever tasted.

Quickly we filled small jars and took them to all the guests to refill their cups. As they each tasted the new fruit of the vine their eyes gleamed and their smiles widened. If there had been gladness before, it was all the more renewed. As the psalmist said, "Their mouths were filled with laughter and their tongues with shouts of joy."

And no one knew what had happened—not the bridegroom, not the master of the feast, not my master and mistress. Only Mary and her son and his friends.

When I had a moment to catch my breath, I looked over to where they were sitting. Mary was smiling quietly; I would even say triumphantly. Her son was eating and drinking as if nothing special had happened. His friends—now they looked as if they had seen a miracle. They were staring at Jesus in bewilderment.

Myself? I am a servant. I know that sounds like a copout, but it says it all for me. I didn't have time to do much thinking at the feast. That breather I took was just that—a breather. The feast only got livelier after the miracle, and I had a lot of cups and plates to keep refilling. When it was over, I was exhausted. Even then I had to wake early the next day for the cleanup. I have not had much time to ponder the miracle.

But this much I can say. Should there be another time to take orders from Jesus of Nazareth, be sure that I will obey without hesitation. Indeed, if I were to encounter a dilemma again, he is the one I would go straight to for help. I respect his mother, Mary. I am in awe of her son.

This is a man worthy to be served. How I wish it could be that he were my master. I would follow him anywhere, serve him however he would have me serve. I understand the role of a servant. It is to obey. It is good to understand as much as possible the business of my master, to be as wise and discerning as I can be. But it is obedience that demonstrates not merely respect for but, more to the point, trust in one's master. It is obedience that a master values most in his servant. An obedience that takes orders, yes, but also an obedience that is in tune with his master's will. And an obedience that is carried out gladly without shame.

I cannot say that I obeyed Jesus gladly. Certainly I felt foolish. But that was before I knew him. Now I know him. It would be my honor to hear him say to me some day, "Well done, good and faithful servant."

The Woman at the Well

And he had to pass through Samaria. So he came to a town of Samaria called Sychar, near the field that Jacob had given to his son Joseph. Jacob's well was there; so Jesus, wearied as he was from his journey, was sitting beside the well. It was about the sixth hour.

A woman from Samaria came to draw water. Jesus said to her, "Give me a drink."

—John 4:4–7

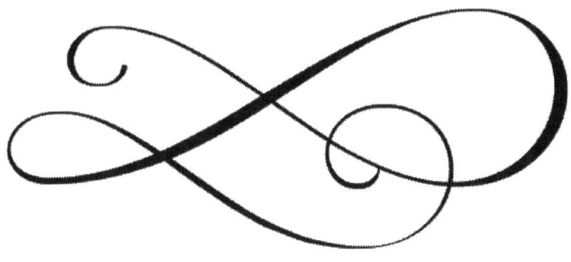

For Full Story:
John 4:4–43

I was wary of him from the start. What was he, a Jew, doing here at Sychar in Samaria? Why was he alone? And why would he not move when he saw me? I had come to the well to draw water, and he would not move but sat there beside it. He knew that he should have stepped away so that I could draw water from it. He knew the code of our culture.

To add to his impertinence, he spoke to me. Yes, he a man spoke to me a woman right out in the open. He did not know me, and yet he spoke. Was he showing his disdain for us Samaritans that he would so flagrantly violate the cultural codes? Such arrogance! Who did he think he was?

It was the noon hour. Already the day was hot. I had to come out alone in the heat of the day to draw my water. Those other women…well, anyhow, I was not in the best of moods on that day. I rarely was.

"Give me a drink of water." Excuse me? Yes, I know how reasonable such a request would seem, but he knew better. He was not observing any of the rules that every person knows. He should have stepped away when I came. He should not have been looking at me. And he should not have been asking anything of me. I would have offered some water. I knew my duties, even if he was a Jew. But I am not some shy, timid, little woman, who can be so easily intimidated. I challenged him.

"How is it that you, a Jew, ask for a drink from me, a woman of Samaria?" Who did he think he was that he could walk onto my territory and boss me around like a servant girl? I was not going to take any lip from this stranger.

Then his arrogance really came out. "If you knew the gift of God, and who it is that is saying to you, 'Give me a drink,' you would have asked him, and he would have given you living water."

Was he a fool? He was taking me for a fool. Living water—there was no spring, definitely no river. Was he going to make it bubble out of the ground? Was he going to turn the well water into spring water? If I knew who was speaking to me—did he think he was the gift of God? I had heard better lines than that before. So like a Jew, thinking that he was better than me because of his religion. Jacob was our father too. He dug this very well. I reminded him of that. I let him know that I knew the Torah. He might think I was some ignorant pagan, but he was challenging the wrong woman.

He ignored my retort. "Everyone who drinks of this water will be thirsty again, but whoever drinks of the water that I will give him will never be thirsty again. The water that I will give him will become in him a spring of water welling up to eternal life."

Now I was getting angry. Give up the joke. And then I looked at his face. His eyes met mine. He was not joking; he was in earnest. He was not looking at me with disdain; he looked with compassion. It unnerved me. He might be a fool; he was not regarding me as a fool. So I responded as though he were serious. I even spoke respectfully: "Sir, give me this water, so that I will not be thirsty or have to come here to draw water." I don't know what I expected him to say or do. What could he?

He made a smart move. He wanted me to get my husband. Nice dodge. I knew what he was up to. I was to go fetch my husband while he slipped away.

"I have no husband." That was the truth, not that he needed to know more. It was one time that my awkward situation served me well. My convenient truth checked his attempt to get out of the awkward place I had put him in. Where was that living water?

But he was off the subject of water. He was no longer interested in our verbal game. His next remark was a low blow, and I might have gone into a rage had I not been astonished by his information.

"You are right in saying, 'I have no husband'; for you have had five husbands, and the one you now have is not your husband. What you have said is true."

How did he know this? I was astonished and embarrassed. Possibly he could have deduced my moral state by the fact of my coming to the well late in the day, but how did he know the details?

I had to think. Why does he even bring this up? Probably he wants to shame me. Maybe he wants to take advantage of me. What am I to do? I steadied myself. I have been in similar predicaments and gotten out of all of them. Then it came to me.

"Sir, I perceive that you are a prophet. Our fathers worshiped on this mountain, but you say that in Jerusalem is the place where people ought to worship."

Flattery works with any man, and nothing gets a Jew off track better than theology. This will set him off. And it seemed to work.

"Woman, believe me, the hour is coming when neither on this mountain nor in Jerusalem will you worship the Father. You worship what you do not know; we worship what we know, for salvation is from the Jews." Just where I wanted him to go, putting us Samaritans down again. I was opening my mouth to argue back, but he continued on.

"But the hour is coming, and is now here, when the true worshipers will worship the Father in spirit and truth, for the Father is seeking such people to worship him. God is spirit, and those who worship him must worship in spirit and truth."

He was in earnest. He was not angry; he was not taunting me. He was inviting me to be a worshiper, just as he had been inviting me to drink his living water. I could see the compassion in his eyes. Again I was unnerved. I could not think of a reply, and so I fell back on an old line that everyone used when they were losing a theological argument.

"I know that Messiah is coming. When he comes, he will tell us all things." He had angered me when he first spoke to me. He had embarrassed me with his revealing information. And yet he had spoken without judgment, without arrogance, even as though he wanted good for me. I had had plenty of experience with men who wanted to get something from me, but here was a man that I could now see was not toying with me and certainly not propositioning me. Here was a man who feared God and wanted me to know his God. My mind was confused.

"I who speak to you am he."

I stared at him. He was serious. He was not joking, just as he had not been joking about living water. The Messiah? Just look at him! Looking at him is what kept throwing me off guard. Here was a man of God who knew everything about me, who ought to have condemned me, but was inviting me to receive his living water and to worship God with him. Could it be true? Could he be the Messiah?

At this moment his followers walked up, and I ran back to town. I cried out, "Come, see a man who told me everything I ever did. Could this be the Messiah?" And do you know what happened? They listened to me! They came with me. They listened to him. They even invited him to stay with them, and he did! For two whole days he stayed and taught us—he a Jew and we Samaritans. And many of my townspeople actually believed him!

How could all of this have happened? He won our hearts as if we were a harvest ripe for reaping. His wise words and his compassion for his enemies whom he treated seriously as fellow worshipers of God—they broke through our defenses.

Me? I did ask for that living water that the Messiah offered, and it has quenched my thirst for love and for acceptance. A new life has sprung up in me—eternal life, a life in which I now worship my Father in spirit and in truth.

The Leper

And a leper came to him, imploring him, and kneeling said to him, "If you will, you can make me clean." Moved with pity, he stretched out his hand and touched him…

—Mark 1:40–41

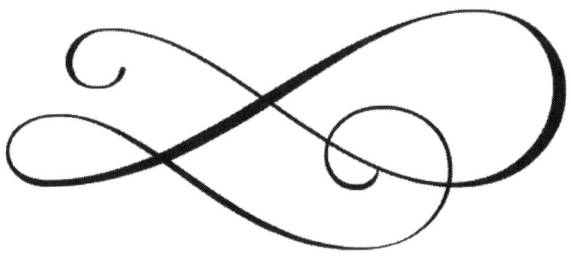

For full story:
Mark 1:40–45

He touched me. He literally touched me! He stretched out his hand and actually touched me! You may wonder what was so wondrous about a touch. Jesus touched lots of people. But I was a leper! A leper!

Let me back up. It was a number of years ago that leprosy first afflicted me. Before then I had a family. One morning I woke up to find spots on my arms. You can imagine my consternation. I kept them covered that day, hoping they would fade away, but next morning they were still there. I showed them to my wife. We agreed that I would go to the local priest and show them to him. He was kind and did not immediately quarantine me as the law prescribed. I was to come back next week to be re-examined. The spots not only remained but clearly had penetrated my skin. The verdict was unavoidable—I must be declared a leper!

Do you understand the horror of such a verdict? To be diagnosed with any other illness is nothing compared to this. I was not sick. I was unclean! Here is what the law says about one such as I.

> The leprous person who has the disease shall wear torn clothes and let the hair of his head hang loose, and he shall cover his upper lip and cry out, "Unclean, unclean." He shall remain unclean as long as he has the disease. He is unclean. He shall live alone. His dwelling shall be outside the camp.

I had to abandon my home, my family. I could not live with them nor they come and live with me. I was contagious—not so much my disease but my uncleanness. To touch me, simply to come near me would make you unclean before the law—the law of God. I was banned from the temple. I could attend synagogue if I stayed behind a screen separated from everyone else, although it was made clear that I was not welcomed.

And why should I be welcomed? I was accursed of God. My leprosy was judgment for my sins. Everyone knew that. The outer uncleanness revealed the filth that was inside me.

As time went on I understood that I was not welcomed in the town. But where could I go? I couldn't even become a mere beggar on the side of the road. No one would come near. Even if they pitied me, they could not stop. To do so would make them unclean. I lived off of scraps left near a little camp occupied by fellow lepers. If I ventured out, I had to warn anyone who might come near that I was unclean. Over the years, I ventured out less and less until my only steps were to get food at the drop off site. I lived the life by which I was labeled—an outcast from society, from all that was considered clean and holy.

Oh, yes, definitely from what was holy. My contagion was bad enough in that it made everything clean unclean by touch or association. But to touch what was holy, I don't know what would happen, only that it would be bad for me and whatever had been holy. Cut off! That is the term used for both of us. I don't know how I could have been more cut off than I was, unless by death. As to what was holy, it would be contaminated and could no longer be associated with God. The unclean touching the holy—it simply was not to be done.

Well, word had gotten out about Jesus of Nazareth. He was some kind of miracle-worker, including healing. Word was that he could heal anyone. Crowds were coming to him and he turned no one away. Would he? Could he cleanse a leper? Maybe if I could get in earshot and call out to him—maybe he would respond? But no, he is not just a miracle worker; he is supposed to be a prophet—a man of God. Why would he help someone who is accursed by the Holy God?

It seemed a foolish idea, but then he was traveling in the area. I at least wanted to see this extraordinary man. I knew a small hill outside a neighboring town. I could stand on it and watch him from a safe distance. Sure enough, the villagers were crowded about him. One man had been carried on a litter and placed in front of him. I could not hear, but I did see him hold out his hand to the man who apparently had no use of his legs. The man stood up as though Jesus was merely offering a hand to a healthy man. I think he must have healed a blind person. Other illnesses I could not tell, but the reaction of the observers and the persons healed signified some kind of miracle. I was especially moved by a woman whose bizarre behavior indicated demon possession. I could hear her screams, then she fell down, and again, Jesus reached out his hand and lifted her up as though from a nap. He could heal, and he was healing everyone. Oh, I yearned to be among them and to receive my own healing.

At dusk, Jesus began to leave the village with what appeared to be followers of his. The road he chose led past my hill. I started to back away out of sight, but it tore at my heart for such a healer to pass my way and I not even try to appeal to his mercy. I knew my chances were slight, since he was a holy man, but what could happen other than a refusal? I had lost shame years ago.

And so, as he drew near, I ran down the hill. I didn't need to call out "unclean!" as my filthy appearance made clear my condition. I didn't even stop at a distance, as I should have. I ran up to him, dropped on my knees, and said, "If you are willing, you can make me clean."

So what would it be? I could hear protests from his followers. Some were yelling at me to get away; others were warning Jesus to back away. The only thing I did not have to fear was anyone laying hands on me to pull me away.

I did not see what was happening, for my head was bowed to the ground. I could hear feet shuffling as people backed away, and the grumbling died down until there was silence. I dared not look up. If Jesus walked away, I could bear it, but I did not want to see the disgust on his face. And then came the touch. I felt a gentle hand on my head and the relief-filling words, "I am willing." And more—the miraculous healing words, "Be clean."

Just a touch from a gentle hand, just words from a kind voice. I lifted my head and looked on his face. He held out his hand and lifted me up. I looked at my arms which were as fresh looking as ever. I looked into his eyes and saw that he saw a man made clean and accepted by God. The curse was removed.

The one time he looked stern was to charge me not to tell anyone. (Not tell anyone?) I was to do as the law instructed, which was to show myself to the priest and make the prescribed offering. That I was willing to do, as it allowed me back into society and to be with my family once again. But not to tell anyone of what Jesus had done for me? How could I keep from testifying to how I had been made clean? How could I refrain from telling others how Jesus was willing to touch me and make me clean? The holy touches the unclean, and instead of either one of us being cut off from God, I am made whole.

I did go to the priest and give my offering. It was a lamb, as the law prescribes. The lamb was killed and placed on the altar as an offering. The priest took blood from the lamb and placed some on my right ear, my right thumb, and my right big toe. He then pronounced me clean. But I knew what really had made me clean. It was the touch of the one willing to touch me when I was unclean, the Holy One who took the risk of becoming a curse to remove my own.

The Paralytic

And they came, bringing to him a paralytic carried by four men. And when they could not get near him because of the crowd, they removed the roof above him, and when they had made an opening, they let down the bed on which the paralytic lay.

—Mark 2:3–4

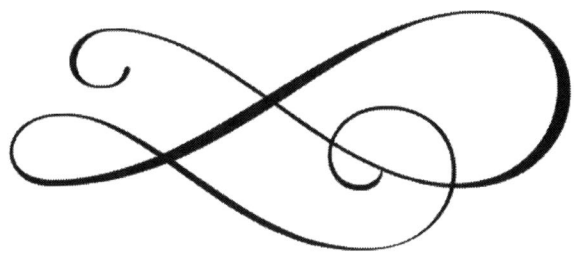

For full story:
Mark 2:1–12

I was embarrassed by the whole episode. Until the moment of healing, all I felt was shame, bitterness, and confusion.

I was a paralytic, a cripple with useless legs. Were it not for my friends, I would have been a beggar in the street pleading for alms. I was not always like this. I was a strong man. "The glory of young men is their strength," says the proverb. I gloried in the strength of my arms and my legs. I gloried in them until the day that the rocks crashed down from the mountainside and robbed me of my glory.

Why me? What had I done that God would punish me so? My friends with me escaped by inches. Only I was crushed. Why? My friends have stood by me. Like Job's friends they have mourned with me. Unlike his friends, they never condemned me even as I railed against God, I suspect out of guilt that they escaped my tragedy.

Why me? Why not them? I was not known as a very devout man, but then neither were they. All of us were good men, I mean good enough men morally. We all kept up our religious duties well enough. Why was I singled out? Eventually, I gave up the useless questions. "Why me?" can be asked only so long before becoming noxious to me and the four men who have stayed by my side.

Routine eventually kicked in. My friends would take turns coming to my small place to care for me and bringing food. What would I have done without them? My parents have died. I have no close family. But as much help that they were, my friends could not pull me out of the deep depression I sank in. The long tedious hours of nothing to do; the position of always being the one helped; the watching young men freely walk about, using their strength to wait on my useless body. They dared not be too happy in front of me, though they tried to lift my spirits.

They knew what I knew, that my accident was no accident. Some sin, something wrong that I had done, must have moved God to punish me. Something about me, something that separated me from them, caused God to single me out.

Then news started to come in. There was a miracle-worker in Galilee, Jesus of Nazareth, who was healing everyone who came to him. Everyone— the sick, the blind, even lepers, even the lame. My friends were beside themselves with excitement. They wanted to take me to this man sent from God.

I may shock you as I shocked them. "If this Jesus is from God, he can find me. God had no trouble finding me to make me his victim." Could I seriously refuse help? You don't know what an embittered man can do. I had spent a great deal of effort digging for myself a pit of pity and bitterness. I was not about to come out of it.

The problem for a crippled man with faithful friends is that he cannot stop what they have determined to do. Permission or no, they picked up my bed and proceeded to carry me down the road to Capernaum, where this miracle-man was staying.

I pleaded with them not to do it. I had not been out in public since taken home from the accident. I was ashamed to be seen. Now my so-called friends are parading me through the streets. I covered myself with my blanket.

The humiliation got worse. They arrived to find a mob around Jesus' house. They could not get near the door. They put me down and conferred with one another. Then, without saying a word to me, they picked up my bed, carried me around the house to a set of stairs leading to the top. "What are you doing?" I yelled at them. The climb itself was nerve-wracking. One misstep and I would be tossed over the side of the stairs. And people were staring, no doubt as perplexed as I by my friends' actions.

They get to the top and lower me. Then, without hesitation, begin to dig through the roof. "Are you mad?" I screamed at them. They ignored me. They steadily worked away, creating an opening. I could hear a commotion below. No wonder. Before I could protest more, they lowered me down.

Never have I felt more shame as all eyes stared at me. I looked about. By their clothing, I recognized Pharisees and scribes in the room. And then

I saw Jesus. I did not have to be told who he was. His presence dominated everyone else. He looked at me briefly with wonder. Then he looked up at my friends and did the strangest thing. He smiled. I think he even laughed. He was clearly pleased with what they had done.

I suppose it was rather funny, wasn't it? I have to admit that I now anticipated what would happen next. He was going to heal me. My friends, everyone in the room waited for the words, "Rise up and walk."

"Take heart, my son; your sins are forgiven." What? My sins are forgiven? I did not say what I was thinking: "I did not come to be forgiven; I came to be healed."

Again, commotion among the crowd. The religious leaders were whispering to one another loud enough. "This is blasphemy. Who does this man think he is? Only God can forgive sins."

Oh great, now I am the exhibit for a religious controversy. I just want to go home, but I am stuck on the floor, my friends in the ceiling, entrapped in a room where my supposed healer is more concerned for my sins than my body. Was this his copout? Was paralysis not on the list of healings he could manage?

And what is it about *my* sins? Am I the only sinner in the room? What did I do to deserve my paralysis? What have I done to deserve being made a spectacle of now?

Speaking over my head to the grumblers, Jesus asked, "Which is easier, to say, 'Your sins are forgiven you,' or to say, 'Rise and walk'?" Then he looked down at me, looked into my eyes while still speaking, "But that you may know that the Son of Man has authority on earth to forgive sins, I say to you, rise, take up your bed and go home."

Power ran through my body into my legs. I could not help but stand up. I did not wobble, I felt no pain, no weakness, I stood up as though I had never been paralyzed. I stood up astonished as everyone else in the room, and without a word I did exactly what Jesus told me to do. I picked up my bed, turned to the door—the crowd parted like the Red Sea—and I walked out.

My friends met me outside. We embraced; we shouted; I jumped about like a little child without any sense of shame. And then we made our way home, my friends trying to keep up with me.

That night, alone at home, I reflected on what Jesus said to me. He asked which was easier to say—"your sins are forgiven" or "rise up and walk." I think his real question for me is which is more important—to be healed of soul or of body? I still cannot think of what sin led to my accident. But it would not be difficult to identify the sins of my heart in that room with him: the self-pity, the resentment, the bitterness that I had been holding against God, even the resentment against my faithful friends for being healthy friends.

Yes, my friends. It was after looking at them, not me, that Jesus pronounced my forgiveness. It was their faith, their determination, that moved him so. Faith in him, love for me.

The Invalid at the Pool

One man was there who had been an invalid for thirty-eight years. When Jesus saw him lying there and knew that he had already been there a long time, he said to him, "Do you want to be healed?"

—John 5:5–6

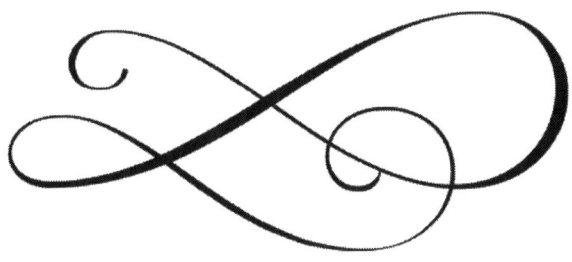

For full story:
John 5:1–47

To be truthful, my life was not all that bad. I had grown used to it long ago while still a young boy. My parents would carry me down to the pool of Bethesda in the morning and come back for me before evening. My mother would pack a lunch for me. After my parents were gone I had friends who would carry me down.

It wasn't a bad life. We formed a little community at the pool, all those of us who lay there. Bethesda has long been a place for the invalid. Its water has been touted for its healing powers. Occasionally, the waters stir. Tradition says that angels stir the water. Maybe, who am I to say otherwise. Stirred or not, many have dipped in the waters, and I have seen a few over time get stronger. Some, getting into the water when stirred, have claimed they were miraculously healed. Possibly, though I have never seen what I'd call a true miracle.

As I said, we formed a little community, watching out for one another, sharing food, though rarely the alms we received. We passed the day begging but also telling stories and sharing news. After thirty-eight years I had become one of the elder statesmen. As I said, it wasn't a bad life.

And then this man comes along I'd never seen before. I didn't take much notice of him at first, though he was behaving a bit odd. Most people pass through quickly to wherever they are going. They don't care to be around us. Some take the time to give out alms as their religious duty. But this fellow hung about and yet gave no alms. I saw him look over at me as he queried another invalid. He was evidently asking about me.

He comes over, looks me over, and then asks, "Do you want to be healed?"

What an odd question. I cannot make him out. He apparently has learned how many years I have been here. I suppose that he is wondering how I can have been here so long and not be healed by the water. So I humor him and play to his pity.

"Sir, I have no one to put me into the pool when the water is stirred up, and while I am going another steps down before me."

I expect him to give me alms. Instead, he simply stares at me. Then he speaks, or rather, he commands me. "Get up, take up your bed, and walk."

Either the man is mad, or he suspects me of being a freeloader, that I am faking my condition. But as I am thinking all this over, I feel a sensation in my legs. These legs that have been useless for nearly forty years are tingling with sensation. I move them. And then I do the most miraculous thing: I obey his command. I stand up.

I expect…well, I'm not sure what I expect. The man just stares at me as though what else was I to do but obey. I feel embarrassed as I look around at all the staring eyes of my friends. Not knowing what else to do, I complete his command. I stoop down, pick up my mat, and walk away. But not far. Before I leave the pool, I turn around. I realize that I have yet to thank him, still somewhat in shock over what has happened. But when I do, I find that he is gone. I hear the voices of my friends congratulating me. I wave to them and leave. I head back to my little room.

I was near home when some men stopped me. I recognized them as belonging to the Pharisees. "What are you doing carrying your bed on the Sabbath?" Thirty-eight years, thirty-eight years lying on the ground and in a few minutes of walking I get into trouble. I explained that I had just been healed. You would think that would have impressed them. After all, I am a walking miracle, Sabbath or no Sabbath. They just frowned. They wanted to know the man's name, not the man who miraculously healed me but the man who commanded me to carry my bed on the Sabbath.

I thought of some choice replies, but I saw in their faces that they could cause me trouble with the authorities. I told them honestly that I did not know who he was. They stared at me. "Get on home quickly and do not carry your bed again on the Sabbath. It is against the law." I assured them I would not and hurried past them.

When I got to my small room, the reality hit me. I am walking! I am walking! Praise the Lord Almighty, I am walking! What, with the strange way the stranger acted toward me and then the interrogation by the religious police, I had been rattled and did not come to my senses until alone. But now, now the miracle of God washed over me. I felt like I had plunged into the pool and came out baptized as a new man.

What should I do now? What does the psalmist say? Oh, yes:

> I will offer to you the sacrifice of thanksgiving
>   and call on the name of the Lord.
> I will pay my vows to the Lord
>   in the presence of all his people,
>   in the courts of the house of the Lord,
>   in your midst, O Jerusalem.

And so I headed to the temple to offer my sacrifice of thanksgiving. I had not much but could afford a pigeon. I had to give thanks to the Lord who has saved me.

It was there that I ran into the stranger, or rather, he found me. Again, his greeting was odd. "See, you are well! Sin no more, that nothing worse may happen to you." Before I could answer, he walked away.

Sin no more? What sin was he referring to? Something worse could happen to me? What is that all about? First, the religious police accuse me of sin—for following his command, I might add. Now he accuses me of sin. Hey, I am in the temple offering sacrifice to the Lord. What makes him think I will sin?

I walked about in the temple court and, sure enough, came across the religious police, this time they were talking with what looked like their superiors. I walked over to them. I wanted them to see how dutiful I was to worship at the temple on the Sabbath. I saw that they were looking over at someone. It was the stranger.

"That's the man who healed me and gave me my orders to carry my bed."

With that they walked over to him and questioned him about breaking the law. If his words had struck me strange before, well, it only got stranger. "My Father is working until now, and I am working."

He spoke with the same authoritative tone he had used with me, but this time he did not quickly walk away. He began a speech that must have been building up inside. I can't remember it all, but he kept referring to the Lord, the Holy One of Israel, as his Father, and that he was his son. No, no… he was *the* Son.

It got wild. He the Son only did whatever the Father did and whatever the Father wanted. The Son not only could do miracles like healing me, but he could raise the dead! Oh, and the Father has given the Son the responsibility to judge. It gets wilder. He, the Son, will be the judge at Judgment Day, and he will have the power to grant eternal life.

He sounded like a madman. The Father bears testimony about him through his miracles. And if that were not enough, the Scriptures are about him. Moses wrote about him!

I thought for sure the men would stone him right then and there, and if it had not been for the Roman garrison in the tower above, I believe they would have. They were furious. But he—I learned that his name was Jesus—he stared at them for a moment and then walked away.

I never did thank Jesus for healing me. He left me speechless each time he spoke to me, and I certainly wasn't going to speak up after that little speech. But what do I do with him? His words are the words of a madman, and yet how can he do such a miracle if God were not with him? Am I not myself a testimony that he is from God? What do you do with a such a man who does not fit the expectation of what a man of God ought to be like? He will not fit convention. He demands to be taken on his own terms. What should I do?

The Centurion of Capernaum

Now a centurion had a servant who was sick and at the point of death, who was highly valued by him. When the centurion heard about Jesus, he sent to him elders of the Jews, asking him to come and heal his servant.

—Luke 7:2–3

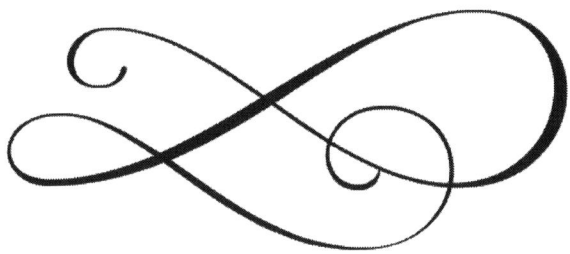

For full story:
Luke 7:1–10

I don't know why anyone should have been amazed by my supposed great faith. My confidence in the Teacher was a matter of deduction, not faith. What required faith was to believe that Jesus would agree to help me.

I am a centurion in the Roman forces that keep order in Palestine. My company is headquartered in Capernaum. My colleagues hate being here. They hate the land and the people. It is dangerous, to be sure, with Zealots lurking about. And the people in general let their resentment be known. Most of the other territories are relatively peaceful. Their people appreciate the improvements we have made in their lands. But for the Jews civic improvements do not compensate being occupied by pagans and blasphemers.

I shared the same feelings of my colleagues when I first came. Unlike my colleagues, though, I took time to learn the people, to discover what motivates them. It is their God. He is unlike the gods of other peoples. He is certainly unlike our gods. He is but one God; there is no other. He is the only Creator, the only sovereign King over all. He is holy, so holy that his people dare not utter his name. No image is allowed to be made of him.

There is but one temple built for him. It stands in Jerusalem. It is his house, though as their famous King Solomon acknowledged, "Will God indeed dwell with man on the earth? Behold, heaven and the highest heaven cannot contain you, how much less this house that I have built!" The temple in Jerusalem is the only place their God will allow them to make sacrifices. It is their holiest site.

Even so, they may worship where they live, and cities and towns have their synagogues. These are houses of worship with prayers, Scripture readings, and exposition. I made the acquaintance of the ruler of the local synagogue, Jairus, and over time he instructed me in the Jewish religion. My intention was to gain better understanding of the people I had to police, but as I learned more my soul was gripped with the majesty of their God and with their concept of righteousness. Their God and their religion, which rules their lives, is far superior, even far more beautiful than the petty gods and rites I have known. I have become what the Jews call a God-fearer.

I have not converted. I have not been circumcised. I am still Gentile, and I have not abandoned my post of a Roman soldier. Nevertheless, I have changed. I worship the one true God. I follow, as best I can, the Scriptures' teachings about justice and righteousness and mercy. I have even helped to build a new synagogue.

Perhaps most importantly is my attitude toward my fellow man. It started with seeing the Jew as a neighbor; seeing my soldiers as individuals, even seeing slaves as human beings. My own servant I came to regard as a son. It was he who led me to seek the help of the Teacher.

I had already known of Jesus. I should have met him, but what with his constant travels and my duties, the opportunity never came up. He had taught in the synagogue a couple of times, the very one I built. Jairus spoke well of him. What Jesus was best known for was his healings, even driving out demons. Jairus told me of how he had ordered a demon out of a man in the synagogue! Jesus would just give orders. "Be healed." "Come out." "Be cleansed."

What was clear was that Jesus possessed authority. He had power, of course, but that power backed up his authority. I understood that. I can fight. My fighting skill is what led to my promotion as centurion. But my men under me obey, not because I can out-fight them but because of my position of authority. They do not fear being challenged to a fight by me, but of the order I could give to discipline them. And so, I say to one, "Go," and he goes; and to another, "Come," and he comes; and to my servant, "Do this," and he does it.

Clearly, Jesus has this same authority, although much greater than mine. He has authority over the natural elements, even over the spiritual world. In my old religion I would have regarded him as a demigod. I'm not sure what to make of him now. The Jews look for the Christ to come, what they call the Messiah. Some rumors are floating about that he is the one. I don't know. He must at least be a prophet like Jairus read to me about from their Scriptures, for clearly his authority was derived from God.

The day came when my servant came down with a fever. I called for doctors, but no one could help. His condition grew worse until it became clear that if nothing was done he would die. Then word came to me. The Teacher is back in town. Jesus, the man of authority, was here. Yes, I knew that he could heal my servant.

I was about to go to him when doubt hit me. I didn't doubt his authority to heal, but it was his authority that made me pause. I would not dare walk into the presence of Caesar without his express permission, and even then without someone to speak on my behalf for that permission. How could I brazenly approach this holy man of God? Others had done so? Yes, but they belonged to the people of God. They were of the chosen race. I might fear God, but I have no claims to his favor. And I remain a soldier. I serve the enemy force, as far as the Jews are concerned. My very presence desecrates their land. How then, could I go before this man's face for mercy?

But my servant was dying. What could I do? I turned to elders of the synagogue. Would they go for me? Would they represent me? They were willing, thank their holy God. They would ask him to come. I sat by my servant and waited and prayed.

But another doubt. What am I asking? To come into my home. That's like asking Caesar to come into my house like a servant to do my bidding. What would Jesus think? I should have had my servant carried to him. But he's too sick. I don't know that he would survive.

I sent some friends. Maybe they could catch the elders before they reached Jesus. All I am asking is for Jesus to give the word, the order of healing. I do the same thing all the time. I send one soldier to another soldier with an order and that second soldier obeys. I don't need to be present to exercise my authority. In the same way, I knew Jesus could do the same. Just give the word, if he would.

It was then that my faith was tested. Would this holy man of God show mercy? Would he listen to an unclean Gentile Roman soldier?

I sat down again by my servant and waited and prayed. It was not long, less than an hour when my servant opened his eyes. I felt his head. His fever was gone. He sat up and asked for food. He was healed.

I am told by the elders and my friends that Jesus marveled over my faith. "Not even in Israel have I found such faith," he said. I am sure that there are many of the chosen people with greater faith than mine. As I said, it doesn't take much faith to believe that a man of authority can give orders for his will to be done.

I marvel that he possessed the will to be merciful to one as unworthy as I.

John the Baptist

The disciples of John reported all these things to him. And John, calling two of his disciples to him, sent them to the Lord, saying, "Are you the one who is to come, or shall we look for another?"

—Luke 7:18–19

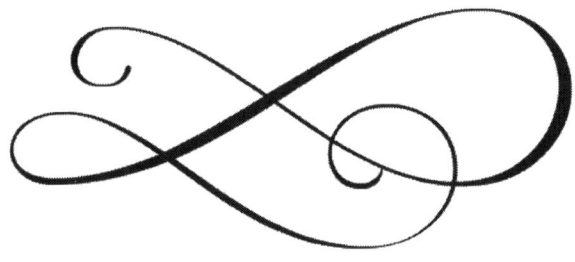

For full story:
Luke 7:18–23

I baptized Jesus reluctantly. I had a clear commission—prepare the way of the Lord's coming by preaching repentance. The baptisms were for sinners repenting and turning back to God. Here then was the Lord standing before me to be baptized. I protested, but he was resolute, explaining that he must fulfill all righteousness. I did not understand but nevertheless obeyed. That is when the sign came upon him, the dove, and I knew he was the Expected One, the Anointed, for here he was being anointed by the Holy Spirit in my presence.

How do I know it was the Spirit of God? I am a prophet of God. It was the Spirit of God who had told me to look for this very sign. I had no doubt that Jesus of Nazareth, born of my mother's cousin Mary, was the Messiah sent by God. I knew that he was the light of the world for which I had been sent to bear witness of.

He soon left, led away by the same Holy Spirit into the wilderness. I too had been led into the wilderness for preparation of my calling. I knew he would return, and when that day would come, my words about the kingdom of heaven would be fulfilled. My baptism was but of water. He would also baptize but with the Holy Spirit himself and with fire.

Yes, the Expected One would return, then would come the real baptism. I had given due warning. My people had long awaited the coming of the Messiah. The greater our oppression, the more intense was the longing. We prayed for the Anointed One to be sent by God to throw off our oppressors and to re-establish God's kingdom in our land. Once again a Son of David would sit upon the throne of a united Israel.

That is what the people longed for; that is what they expected. But they did not understand all that the Lord's coming entailed. His coming meant the Day of Judgment. They, of course, did expect judgment, but it was a judgment for the oppressors. We could be called a people of oppression, given how much of our history has been taken up with foreign invaders. O, we have longed for the Messiah to end oppression for good and for God to rain down judgment upon all foreign enemies.

I too looked for such judgment, but I knew that judgment would begin with the very chosen nation of God. I knew that our oppression through the years was the result of our own sins. For time and time again we turned from serving our covenant God. I knew well Malachi's prophecy: "For behold, the day is coming, burning like an oven, when all the arrogant and all evildoers will be stubble. The day that is coming shall set them ablaze, says the Lord of hosts, so that it will leave them neither root nor branch." Yes, I had meditated on those words many times during my preparation in the wilderness. I knew that judgment was not reserved for the wicked Gentiles alone, but that even within the very covenant people of God were the arrogant and evildoers.

As God's covenant people, we were to be a kingdom of priests and a holy nation. Judgment must begin with us who had failed to live up to our calling. And so I preached to my people to repent. Turn now from sin while there is time. Turn your hearts to the Lord now. Be cleansed from your sins. That is what my baptism was about. I called sinners to repent, and those who heard and were convicted, who were ready to turn from their sin and live for God, came to be baptized as a sign of their new change. Through their turning to the Lord God, I was preparing the way for the Lord who is the Anointed One to come for his mission.

I knew early on that I was the fulfillment of prophecy. When the religious leaders demanded to know who I was, I told them: "I am the voice of one crying out in the wilderness, 'Make straight the way of the Lord.'" I was that voice that Isaiah spoke of. I was the Elijah that Malachi said would be sent forth to prepare for this great day. I was the friend of the bridegroom preparing for his wedding day. Far from being jealous, I rejoiced in his coming. He must increase, and I must decrease.

And so, when I was arrested, I did not despair. All of God's prophets have suffered for speaking his word. Why should I expect to be different?

Besides, I easily could see how my departure made room for the Messiah. For that matter, how long could my imprisonment be? The prophet Isaiah prophesied that the Messiah would set prisoners free!

I then waited patiently for the prison doors to open and for judgment on God's enemies to pour forth. But no judgment came, no baptism of fire. My own disciples sent me reports. Jesus was preaching about the kingdom of God drawing near. Good. But where is that kingdom? He seems content to simply preach about it. Yes, I heard about the miracles. Very good, but where were the signs of judgment? He was doing nothing more than Moses or Elijah or Elisha had done. Now they had produced real signs—plagues, fire from heaven, curses that brought death. Where was the baptism of fire from Jesus?

I sent disciples to inquire of him: "Are you the one who is to come, or shall we look for another?" I knew what I had been sent by God to do. I was to prepare the way for the Messiah. Did I mistake who that Messiah was? Was he still to come?

I waited for a reply. Many days went by before my disciples returned. They told me what had been reported before, but this time they had witnessed the miracles of healing and the preaching. Again, this was nothing new, but then one of my disciples repeated the message, word by word, that Jesus gave for me: "the blind receive their sight and the lame walk, lepers are cleansed and the deaf hear, and the dead are raised up, and the poor have good news preached to them. And blessed is the one who is not offended by me."

Yes, I understood whom that last remark was aimed at. It irked me. Even so, I contemplated the message. Why those words? And then I realized his message, or rather, his reference. He was signaling to me the prophecy of Isaiah, the same prophet who had spoken of me.

> Then the eyes of the blind shall be opened,
>   and the ears of the deaf unstopped;
> then shall the lame man leap like a deer,
>   and the tongue of the mute sing for joy.
> The Spirit of the Lord God is upon me,
>   because the Lord has anointed me

> to bring good news to the poor;
>> he has sent me to bind up the brokenhearted,
> to proclaim liberty to the captives,
>> and the opening of the prison to those who are bound;
> to proclaim the year of the Lord's favor.

But the next line of the prophecy speaks of the vengeance of our God. Why not add that line? Why not the judgment? Where is the judgment?

As I contemplated, my own prophesy came back to me, a phrase I had uttered soon after baptizing Jesus. "Behold, the Lamb of God, who takes away the sin of the world!" Where did those words come from? They did not match what I had been proclaiming about the Messiah. If I was ever carried along by the Holy Spirit, it was in speaking those words. What did they mean? Lamb of God? When was that ever said of the Messiah? I thought again of Jesus' reference to Isaiah. Yes, of course, the answer was in Isaiah.

> Surely he has borne our griefs
>> and carried our sorrows;
> yet we esteemed him stricken,
>> smitten by God, and afflicted.
> But he was pierced for our transgressions;
>> he was crushed for our iniquities;
> upon him was the chastisement that brought us peace,
>> and with his wounds we are healed.
> All we like sheep have gone astray;
>> we have turned—every one—to his own way;
> and the Lord has laid on him
>> the iniquity of us all.

The judgment. Am I to understand that the judgment is to fall on the Messiah? The Anointed One is the sacrificial Lamb? I quietly await whatever may come. Surely God's word through Isaiah is true:

> My thoughts are not your thoughts,
>> neither are your ways my ways.
> For as the heavens are higher than the earth,
>> so are my ways higher than your ways
>> and my thoughts than your thoughts.

Simon the Pharisee

One of the Pharisees asked him to eat with him, and he went into the Pharisee's house and reclined at table. And behold, a woman of the city, who was a sinner, when she learned that he was reclining at table in the Pharisee's house, brought an alabaster flask of ointment, and standing behind him at his feet, weeping, she began to wet his feet with her tears and wiped them with the hair of her head and kissed his feet and anointed them with the ointment.

—Luke 7:36–38

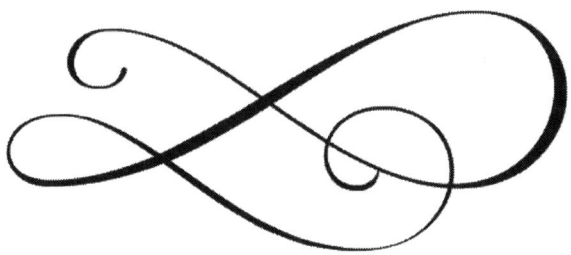

For full story:
Luke 7:36–50

Lack of courtesy? Jesus accuses *me* of lacking courtesy? Let's list his acts of outright rudeness. What guest publicly insults his host? What guest publicly honors a notorious sinner over his host? What guest publicly encourages scandal in his host's home?

Lack of courtesy. The nerve! I kept my thoughts to myself. I did not embarrass him. He was making a scandalous fool of himself without any word from me. I ought to have rebuked him. I ought to have had the woman thrown out immediately. How did my servants let her get inside the courtyard? I will find out, to be sure.

Lack of courtesy. What was it I neglected to do? Oh, yes. I gave him no water for his feet. That is not my fault. I will be sure to punish the servant who had that responsibility. I cannot keep up with everyone and their duties. I will speak to my steward. Why criticize me? I am the host, not the steward. I have already many responsibilities. I had many other guests, not counting his little pack of disciples. If he needed water, why didn't he ask for it?

What's next? I gave him no kiss. I was busy with other guests. I did not know that he would be so sensitive about such things. Look, the very fact that I had him in my home for dinner should have made him feel honored. What other Pharisee has invited him into his house? I would have thought that he would be grateful for the invitation. I was risking my own reputation. He should know that.

And then the oil. I did not provide oil for his forehead. Well, again, that is the responsibility of my steward. If I had known that Jesus would take such particular note of such small things, I would have instructed my steward accordingly. But I understood Jesus as not counting such customs of honor important. Isn't he the one always stressing humility? I seem to recall him criticizing my brethren for wanting to be taken notice of.

He turns out to be the typical peasant religious fanatic full of spite against those of us who have made something of ourselves, secretly resentful of the honor we have achieved. No doubt that is why he indulged in the pathetic adoration of that sinful woman.

He tries to spiritualize the tawdry scene with one of his quaint parables. A moneylender forgives one debtor 500 denarii and another 50 denarii. Who then will love him more? Why bring up the whole matter? I had not criticized him, not aloud as he seems to think. Why address the question to me? Everyone in the courtyard was scandalized. Why not address it to them all? Why call on me, the host, the one to whom he owed courtesy himself?

Well, I had to answer. Of course the one who owed more. I knew Jesus was setting me up, and he took full advantage of it with the accusations of my supposed transgressions. That is bad enough, but to contrast them with this wicked woman's shameless behavior is too much! He is actually commending her! No respectable woman would dare show her hair much less use it to wipe a man's dirty feet. That she would dare touch him is scandalous enough, but she kisses his feet! And Jesus just reclines on his couch as though it is all proper. I should be commended for keeping my composure, not rebuked in front of my guests.

Oh, and there is the perfume she pours on his feet. What is it with Jesus' feet? If she is going to be recklessly extravagant, then at least put it where it belongs—on his head. I don't even want to think of how she got the money to pay for it, definitely not how she has used it before.

How could Jesus permit this? Don't talk to me about forgiveness. This is about what is proper. I don't really blame the woman. She acts the way she was brought up, no doubt. She is a typical, emotional woman who lets her feelings control her. But Jesus should know better. If there is something going on between the two of them, wait until a private time and a private place.

Love. Which debtor loves the moneylender more, he asked? They are grateful, to be sure, but love? Who loves a moneylender? Why did they get into debt in the first place? Why should they be let off so easily? Will it make them better men? More likely they will pat themselves on the back for their good luck.

That's the fault with Jesus. It is fine and good to throw forgiveness around as though one is God. (Where does he get off thinking that it is his to give?) Forgiveness should not come easily. One must earn forgiveness. Take that woman. She ought to have renounced her lifestyle and after a few years in which she has demonstrated proper remorse and change, then she can seek forgiveness. At that time, if she really has changed, she will know the proper way to act in public and with men.

But she never will change, not that kind of a woman. I know the warning of Solomon.

> And now, O sons, listen to me,
>   and be attentive to the words of my mouth.
> Let not your heart turn aside to her ways;
>   do not stray into her paths,
> for many a victim has she laid low,
>   and all her slain are a mighty throng.
> Her house is the way to Sheol,
>   going down to the chambers of death.

I suppose Jesus meant a dig at me with that remark, "He who is forgiven little, loves little." What was he saying—that I was to make a fool of myself over him? Who is it that I am supposed to love? Does he mean God? Surely not. Who has shown more love for God than I? I fast twice a week; I give tithes of all that I get. Why I tithe even the herbs grown in my garden. I give alms to the poor. I not only study the law, I practice it. And unlike a certain woman, there has been no hint of scandal in my life. What more must I do to prove my love for God?

But really, what is it with this insistence on love? What matters is to fear God, not blubber over him. And this woman, this sinner—if she was so full of love for God, why was she not at the temple? Why was she not offering sacrifice? What does crying over dirty feet have to do with love for God? It is clear that she loves Jesus, no doubt for the cheap forgiveness that he so freely imparts.

"Your sins are forgiven." That comment only added to the scandal in my house. "Who is this, who even forgives sin?" My brothers and I will have a long discussion about that remark. Just who does Jesus think he is? Who does this woman think he is, I wonder?

Finally, after his big speech, Jesus sent her away. "Your faith has saved you. Go in peace." What was he talking about? It was as if he and that sinner had a language that only they could understand? As far the woman was concerned, none of the rest of us existed. She and Jesus were alone. As for Jesus, he acted as though he already knew her, that he already knew her thoughts.

How did faith save her? Save her from what? However much she had lost control of herself, I have to admit, something happened to calm her. I would have thought then that she be embarrassed. She merely strolled peacefully away as though she had not a care in the world.

Shameful. Where is my steward? I cannot allow such a scene in my house again.

The Prostitute

Then turning toward the woman he said to Simon, "Do you see this woman? I entered your house; you gave me no water for my feet, but she has wet my feet with her tears and wiped them with her hair. You gave me no kiss, but from the time I came in she has not ceased to kiss my feet. You did not anoint my head with oil, but she has anointed my feet with ointment."

—Luke 7:44–46

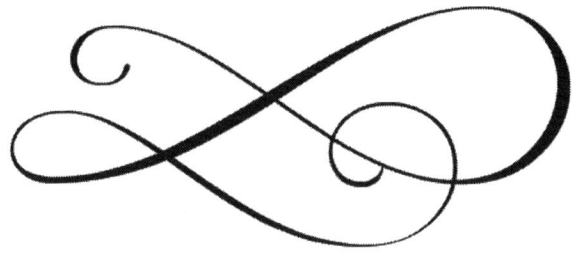

For full story:
Luke 7:36–50

I suppose I made a fool of myself. Surely I scandalized the host and his friends, respected as they are. I did not mean to. Emotion did get the best of me. Perhaps you will understand why.

I am… I was a sinner. I was a prostitute. I will not make excuses claiming poverty forced me into it or that wicked men took advantage of me. Other women have faced more dire circumstances than I and kept from such shame. All I can say is that once I started down that path I followed it completely. And it served me well. I may have been cut off from proper society, but, still, I found another society that did not judge me. I may not have been loved by the men, but then neither was I cursed by them. They gave me nice things besides money—nice clothing, jewels, precious oils. There were other "sinners" for companions. Being made outcasts caused us to form our own community.

It was not such a bad life. There were the disdainful looks of the respectable folks, especially from the Pharisees and scribes who walked by on the other side of the street. There were the women who glared at me and huddled their children close to them as though I preyed upon them. There were the leers, the disgusting grins of men. But for the most part, I was separated from them all. Men came to me.

The worst times were the nights alone in an empty bed with nothing but my thoughts. Memories of a childhood reciting the law, listening to stories from the Scriptures. I idolized the women of faith. There were our mothers of faith—Sarah and Rebecca. Rachel was my ancestor, as I am from the tribe of Benjamin. My father taught me our genealogy. It was painful to think of my father and mother. I loved the story of Samson, how strong and brave he was. Yes, Samson—the irony did not escape me of his attraction to prostitutes. Why it pained me instead of making me smile, well, I kept those thoughts down.

I did my best not to look inside. It was the outside that I focused on, how to keep myself attractive. Oddly enough, it was what Jesus had to say about Pharisees in that regard that broke me down.

I had known Jesus since the dinner Matthew had held for him a year ago. Matthew was a friend of mine. I did not know that it was his farewell party or that he had invited us so that we would meet Jesus. I did not understand then the change that Jesus had made in Matthew's life. We all knew about his miracles and heard that he was a prophet.

At first we thought Matthew had set us up for a fiery denouncement from this prophet. He spoke about the kingdom of God. He was clear enough about the need of repentance, but he did not treat us like we were worse sinners than anyone else. Even the religious folks he included with us as sinners, which brings up another irony.

Matthew's house was similar to the Pharisee's house, and we were reclining at a large table in a courtyard, just like the guests at Simon's dinner. In the same way that I came in uninvited to Simon's home, so some Pharisees and scribes came to Matthew's house.

They were angry, I remember. And though they stood at a distance, they were grumbling to some of Jesus' disciples about his dining with us sinners. Jesus spoke up, like he did now. I remember it well. "Those who are well have no need of a physician, but those who are sick. I have not come to call the righteous but sinners to repentance." If these men had listened earlier, they would know that he considered them also to be sinners. I remember thinking that maybe I was not so bad after all.

I left that dinner intrigued but not changed. I was glad for Matthew, but becoming religious was not for me. Still, I kept an outside interest. Living in Capernaum I came across Jesus teaching on the street or down by the sea. It was always about the kingdom of God, what it is like to belong to it. A couple of times I heard the Pharisees and scribes debating with him. One was just a couple of nights ago. Jesus uttered a rebuke that stung me. "Now you Pharisees cleanse the outside of the cup and of the dish, but inside you are full of greed and wickedness."

He could have turned to me and said the same thing. Indeed, I felt as if he had. Did I imagine it, or did he glance over to me? I lay in bed that night. What was inside of me? What did Jesus see? The greed for money, for good things, for pleasure? Did he see wickedness that hardened me to so glibly transgress the law? Did he see what makeup and rich clothes could not cover? Did he smell the stench that my perfumes could not remove?

My sins marched out before me: the adulteries, the idolatries, the greed, the hatred, and resentment. The coveting, the lying, the stealing. I could not block them. Specific instances paraded before my mind until I felt the disgust by which Jesus, a holy man, must regard me. My tears flowed. I thought of the smirks and the glares of people on the streets, and yet, they had no idea of my real degradation.

The next day I walked along the streets, my head down and covered. A woman's voice called out to me. I looked up. It was a fellow… well, someone in my line of work. And yet she was different. I had not seen her for weeks. Her clothes were plain, but her face—it was…what do I want to say? It was peaceful, and she looked on me with love. She then shared with me how she had been brought before Jesus for judgment and had found forgiveness instead.

Forgiveness? What had she done to earn forgiveness? She didn't know. All she knew was that when she looked into his face she saw pity and mercy. And she heard the words, "Your sins are forgiven."

Could that be true? Could I have my sins forgiven? I returned home, fell on my knees and prayed over and again, "God, have mercy on me, a sinner." My tears flowed. Something was happening inside.

I had to find Jesus. The next day I asked around and learned that he was having dinner with Simon the Pharisee. That would be the last place I'd be welcomed. I must wait for a proper time, a proper place. But when? Where? Where would Jesus go that I would ever be accepted? I cannot wait. I must go now. I should take something with me, something to show honor. I'll take the flask of oil. It's the most expensive possession I have.

I hurry to the house. There they are in the courtyard reclining at the tables. The servants are busy. I can slip in near him before I am noticed. I am behind him now. He looks up at me. I see mercy. My tears flow. I fall at his feet. My tears are falling on them. My hair has fallen down. I use it to wipe off the tears. I am sobbing now from intense relief. I feel as if Jesus were wiping away the heavy weight of my guilt. I kiss his feet. I take the flask and pour the oil over them, and kiss them more.

There is talking. Apparently Jesus is speaking to Simon, but I am not listening. Peace is drowning out words and everything else. But then he sits up, takes my hands, and raises me up. "Your sins are forgiven. Your faith has saved you; go in peace." I look into his eyes, inside of him, and there I see mercy and love. There I find peace.

I can't say what happened next. I must have walked out. I must have walked home. What does happen next? I must leave my life as a sinner, that's to be sure. How will I survive? The words I have heard him speak come back to me. I seem to recall so many of his teachings. "Seek first the kingdom of God and his righteousness, and all these things will be added to you."

What had Jesus said in Matthew's house? He had come to call sinners to repentance. I have heard that call.

A Disciple in the Storm

And a great windstorm arose, and the waves were breaking into the boat, so that the boat was already filling. But he was in the stern, asleep on the cushion. And they woke him and said to him, "Teacher, do you not care that we are perishing?"

—Mark 4:37–38

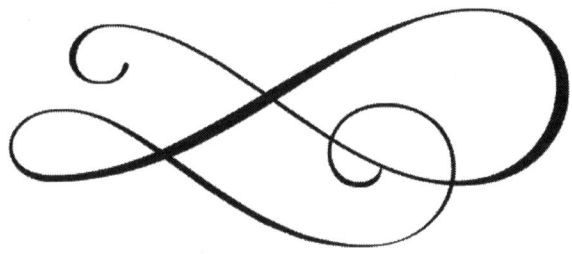

For full story:
Mark 4:35–41

I am still shaken. Yes, shaken by the terror of the storm, but more than that, I am shaken by Jesus.

I am not one of the fishermen. I have never been comfortable in a boat. It had already been a long day of teaching and healing. The crowd was wearying, what with the hot sun bearing down. I followed Jesus to learn from him, not to become a crowd-control worker. It would be fine if Jesus was somehow organizing them for the time that he takes control of the country and sets up his throne. He talks about the kingdom of God, but he doesn't seem to be going anywhere with it. The kingdom is supposed to spring out of the ground somehow. And the healings—that's great and all, but what are they accomplishing other than attracting crowds?

I'm sorry. I know I am sounding negative, but I am still wiped out by what happened. So, near the end of the day, when the sun is going down, Jesus decides that we will cross the lake. I understand waiting, as the winds are their strongest in the afternoon, but crossing the lake at night did not excite me. These fishing boats are built for boating off the coast, not crossing deep water. The one we were to sail on was not large. It could barely hold thirteen men. The sides are not high and with so many of us on board, it was already sitting low in the water. Like I said, I am not a veteran fisherman, but looking at Peter and his fellow boatmen, they did not seem to relish the prospect themselves. But our Teacher is our Master, and true disciples follow their master's orders.

We sailed smoothly halfway across the lake with no trouble. It was actually a pleasant voyage, the air warm with a steady breeze blowing our sail. Jesus had fallen asleep on the stern. He deserved the rest. I thought of closing my eyes as well. Peter and John had the boat under control. And then a gust of wind ruffled the sail. The boat shook. All quieted down. Then a gust again and another gust hitting from the opposite direction. Waves started to lap the boat. Quickly the winds picked up from different directions. The sail strained then ripped. Waves started to overlap the boat; no, they started to pour into the boat.

Peter ordered us to bail water. Andrew and James tried rowing to steady the boat, but it was all to no avail. We could not stay afloat much longer. We had to yell to be heard over the roaring winds and the raging waves. Fear gripped us all. I looked over at Jesus…and he was *sleeping*! He was still sleeping!

I understand the man being tired, but this was absurd! How can one physically sleep on a boat being dashed about by waves and winds? At first I was amazed, but I quickly (I must confess) became angry. How could he sleep at a time like this? We, his disciples, were about to die.

Being nearest to him, I shook him awake. "Master, do you not care that we are perishing?" It wasn't just that he had been sleeping, but that when I woke him he did not seem alarmed. My goodness, he is soaking wet from the waves. He is half submerged in water. We are not in near danger; we are going under now.

Jesus did not respond to me. He grabbed the mast, stood up, and…and scolded the wind. "Peace! Be still!" And the wind ceased, the waves calmed, and the lake became still. Just like that. It was as if angry nature had become embarrassed by Jesus' rebuke.

Well, we were awe-struck; we were relieved; we were exhausted. Our bodies and our nerves had been strained to the limit. We had faced violent death. Then, in a moment all was quiet as though the lake had never been disturbed. We had despaired of help, felt abandoned by our Master, then watched him coolly command the powerful storm to stop, then watched that storm immediately behave.

We stared at him in wonder and in fear. "Who is this, that even wind and sea obey him?" It was then that we could have used some comforting words. "Don't worry, God is watching over us." Something like that, something to calm our nerves. But what does Jesus have to say? "Why are you afraid? Have you no faith?"

What is this? He is rebuking us? Our boat is sinking in a storm and he wants to know why we were afraid? What did he mean rebuking us for lack of faith? In him? He had been asleep! Were we supposed to have waken him earlier? Was that the problem? The storm hit us without warning. Were we supposed to have had faith that the boat would not sink? It was sinking! Were we supposed to have faith to calm the storm ourselves? That was not in the discipleship manual.

Or, was he asking why we were afraid after the miracle? For afraid we were. We thought we knew him. We believed he was the Messiah, the Anointed One come to bring in the kingdom of God and deliver us from the Romans. We believed he was sent from God. We knew he was given power by God to perform miracles. We saw the healings. We saw how he commanded evil spirits to come out of their victims.

But command the forces of nature? To rebuke a mighty storm as if it were a child having a temper tantrum and make it obey? The wind did not die down. It stopped, immediately. The waves did not slowly quiet down, the lake turned calm, immediately.

"Have you no faith?" We thought we were filled with faith in our Master, the Messiah. We had more faith than anyone else. But, I suppose our faith only reached so far. This stilling of the storm is not about using power, but using authority, an authority possessed only by God. Who is he?

No faith. Maybe the problem is not that we haven't enough faith but the wrong faith. Maybe that is why we have failed to make sense of his parables and his teachings. John the Baptist—he could be understood. Repent, get ourselves right with God, and then get ready to join the Messiah's forces when he brings in the kingdom of God. Jesus teaches about the kingdom of God, for sure, but through stories about seeds and teachings about loving one's enemies. What is that about?

And what is his strategy? He recruited us to be his disciples and more have been joining us, but not many. He is drawing crowds, but they are mostly the sick coming to be healed. People listen to his sermons. He preaches with authority. But what is the result? The people return home once they are healed and fed. There is no army being formed, no organizing is being done. We follow him from village to village, and nothing seems to be accomplished other than becoming popular. We spend more time escaping crowds rather than turning them into a useful force.

Jesus is not popular with the religious leaders. It wouldn't hurt if he could somehow enlist them on his side. But he spends his energy rebuking them. The only folks he has not rebuked are the Romans, the oppressors he should be delivering us from.

I have to admit, I've wondered if he lacked the guts. It is one thing to scold the common people. It takes a little more gumption to tweak the noses of the religious leaders. But to confront the Roman occupiers takes courage. Did he lack it? Is that why he skirted the issue, why he even seemed to curry their favor with this foolishness about carrying their packs an extra mile and turning the other cheek?

But the storm—commanding the storm to shut up and sit down. No, this is not a man to be cowered by other mortals. This is not a mere man. Who is he? What is he? It seems this discipleship business will require me to give up my preconceptions of who I am following. I will have to accept this Jesus on his terms and not my own.

The Pig Herdsman

And when he saw Jesus from afar, he ran and fell down before him. And crying out with a loud voice, he said, "What have you to do with me, Jesus, Son of the Most High God? I adjure you by God, do not torment me." For he was saying to him, "Come out of the man, you unclean spirit!" And Jesus asked him, "What is your name?" He replied, "My name is Legion, for we are many."

—Mark 5:6–9

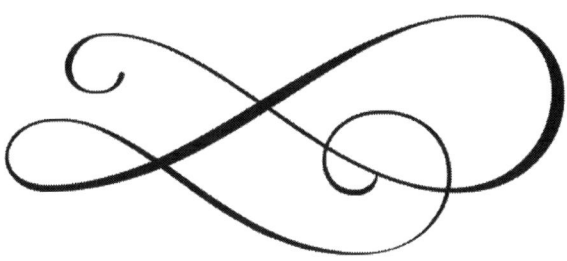

For Full Story:
Mark 5:1–20

Sure we wanted him to leave. He isn't safe!

I saw the whole thing. I was the nearest herdsman when this Jesus shows up on a boat with some other men. Clearly they were strangers, Jews. I wondered what they were doing in Gentile country. They surely did not know the danger of where they were landing. Everyone around here knows about the wild man.

For years he has been demon possessed and like no one else. There are always one or two crazy persons with evil spirits in them, but this man went beyond anything we had ever seen. He called himself in his rantings Legion, and he acted like he had a legion of demons in him. How else to explain his supernatural strength?

He is a dangerous man. I can't say that he's killed a man, but I know that he has killed my pigs. We've expected someday to find that he has killed himself, what with the rages he would go into, clawing his skin and hitting himself with stones. His clothes he had long ago destroyed. It was the blood-curdling screams that most unnerved us. A couple of times we tried to restrain him, even used chains and shackles, but he would break them with his bare hands! For the most part we have stayed away. He lives out among the tombs and usually does not leave, though sometimes he will run out into the wilderness. But he always returns at night. Fortunately, he never comes into the city. He hates company, which is fine with all of us. My fellow herdsmen have to keep fairly near, as our pigs often feed on the hillside next to the tombs. Still, we manage to give him a wide berth. He isn't safe.

Again, this Jesus shows up. I see him and his men coming ashore. My first thought is to give him warning, as they were landing near the tombs. Just as I start to yell out to them, I hear the scream of Legion. Even if I try to yell, the wild man's screams would drown me out. I run as close as I dare, waving my arms, but that is useless. Their eyes are fixed on the screaming man who is running down to them.

Like I said, I have never seen Legion actually kill a man. but I remember well the power with which he struck a couple of men when we had tried to restrain him. He easily could have killed us all, and he looked like he was about to do it now in his rage.

But was I mistaken! He runs directly at this man Jesus and, incredibly, falls on his knees before him. I could hear him. He begs Jesus not to harm him!

"What have you to do with me, Jesus, Son of the Most High God? I beg you, do not torment me."

What did I miss? Jesus had not done a thing. He had picked up no stone. None of the men had weapons. They had no chains. No one was touching him. It was clear that the men with Jesus were terrified themselves. But Jesus, he was different. He stood calm. I could see his face. He did not look like a man trying to keep up his courage. He looked at the demon-possessed wild man as a parent looking at a child throwing tantrums.

He was speaking, not to the man but to the spirits inside. He was commanding them to come out. I realized that it was not the man who was filled with terror but the demons inside him. When had demons ever been afraid of any man?

"What is your name?"

"Legion, for we are many."

Jesus remained calm. I would have run away hearing that demonic voice (or was it voices) were I not myself spellbound by the stranger.

Legion continued as the man groveled before Jesus.

"Do not send us into the abyss!"

What were they talking about? What did they fear? What could this one man do to them?

The wild man looked over at me. No, not me, past me to the hillside to the herd of pigs.

"Send us into them!"

My pigs? What do my pigs have to do with anything? I looked over to them. We had 2,000 at last count. They were blissfully foraging on the hill.

The herdsmen were looking my way, but they were too far away to hear what was being said. I looked back at Jesus and Legion.

"Go," is all Jesus said.

The man shook violently and fell over as though dead. And then I felt the ground shake and the sound of hooves stampeding. I spun around to see the pigs rushing down toward the lake, rushing down into the lake with such force that they piled upon one another. And still they kept coming, pouring into the waters, madly screaming, crushing the animals already dead in the water, using them as a ramp to go deeper to their own deaths. It was a horrible, horrible scene.

I ran. I caught up with the other men, and we rushed to the town. We must have seemed madmen ourselves as we came to the townspeople. "They are all drowned," we were screaming. When we caught our breaths, we explained what had happened, how the pigs had become demon-possessed and stampeded to their deaths.

"It was that man Jesus," I said. "He did it." Then I explained the interaction between Jesus and Legion.

A crowd followed us back. We came first to the gruesome scene of the pigs. The people were horrified. We passed on to where Jesus his men and the wild man had been. They were all still there. The wild man was sitting at the feet of Jesus. Everything was the same as we left it, but everything was different. The wild man was no longer wild. He had been naked, now he was clothed, even clean. When we came up, he stood and smiled at us. He was calm. He was actually in his right mind.

This might sound strange, but seeing the wild man completely changed frightened us all the more. What had this Jesus done to him? Who was this Jesus? You may say that he must be from God to expel the demons. Is that right? I've heard it told that such work can only be done by someone possessed by the prince of demons. Would God have sent the demons into the pigs? This is going to ruin my owners.

Look, we had managed okay without this stranger meddling with our way of life. The wild man was basically controlled. We might lose a pig every now and then, but no other harm was being done. The screams were the worse part, but, like I said, he kept to himself.

And so, like the demons who had begged, we begged Jesus to leave and to leave quickly. After seeing his power, no one was going to try and force him. I suppose the obvious fear in us moved him to get back into his boat. The wild man (I know he is no longer wild, but that is the only way I have known him), he begged Jesus to take him along. That would have been fine with us. But Jesus refused.

"Return to your home, and declare how much God has done for you." Come back to our town? Are we ready for that? He may be calm now but for how long? How can we be sure his change is permanent?

To my surprise some of the townspeople actually welcomed him and took him along with them. Most of us, though, are skeptical and cautious. We will keep chains handy. The pigs—what a mess to clean up. We will have to butcher them and save as much meat as we can. I should have asked Jesus what God has done for me.

One thing for sure, whatever one might claim about Jesus—that he is of God or of the demons—it is clear that he is not safe. When he comes around he will shake up your life. It won't stay the same.

Jairus

Now when Jesus returned, the crowd welcomed him, for they were all waiting for him. And there came a man named Jairus, who was a ruler of the synagogue. And falling at Jesus' feet, he implored him to come to his house, for he had an only daughter, about twelve years of age, and she was dying.

—Luke 8:40–42

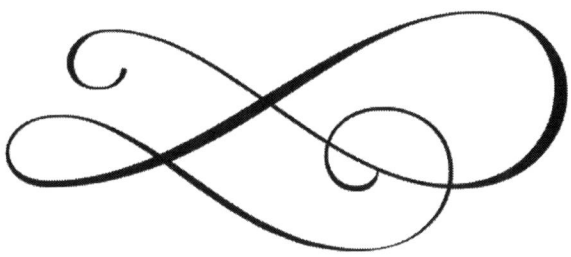

For full story:
Luke 8:40–56

"Child. Arise." Just like that. He takes her lifeless hand and says, "Child, arise." And my daughter rose from her bed as though she had simply been sleeping. How simple. The Teacher could get things done.

That is my job—to get things done, to have everything prepared for worship. I am the ruler of the local synagogue. It is to me that everyone looks for orders and for answers. I see that all is in place; I plan the service and what is needed to support the service. When a guest rabbi comes, I approve his speaking and make all ready for him.

Jesus himself had spoken in my synagogue a number of times. I had been hesitant at first to let him speak in the Seat of Moses. The young self-proclaimed teacher had no credentials, no references. Were it not for his popularity, I would not have gone along with having him. He was a miracle worker supposedly. All the more reason I was wary of him.

But he spoke and, admittedly, with authority that I had not heard the likes of. That was not all. On that very first occasion he drove out a demon in a worshiper. I can assure you that I have never had such a disruption in my services, certainly no demon possessed maniacs. But there it was—a possessed man crying out, "What have you to do with me? I know you are the Holy One of God!"

I was startled, to say the least. I needed to get the madman out of the building, but before I could react, Jesus commanded the spirit to come out of him, and it did. Just like that. I still did not know who this Jesus was, but I could not deny his authority and his ability to get things done.

Over a brief period of time, the Teacher became a celebrity in Capernaum. The Teacher was the Miracle-Worker. Once he even cured the servant of the centurion in charge of the fort outside our border town. Capernaum became a sort of headquarters for Jesus, a home base for his itinerant ministry. One of his disciples was a former tax collector. Matthew was his name. That startled a lot of us. How could a man of God select such a sinner to be his disciple? No reputable rabbi would have done so. But then, we had to admit, Matthew had never been the same. The impudent cohort of the Romans changed. He gave up his practice and followed after this young teacher as ardently as the most devoted, religious disciple. As the centurion noted—a rather godly man himself—the Teacher was a man of authority. If he tells an unclean spirit to depart, it departs. If he calls a notorious sinner to follow him, he follows.

And the Teacher did turn out to be a Miracle-Worker. There seemed to be nothing that he could not do—heal fevers, give hearing to the deaf, make the lame walk, cleanse lepers. No, he had no credentials, but it was obvious that he had God-given power and authority. I had no problem opening the synagogue to him again for teaching the Scriptures.

Capernaum was Jesus' home base, but he was gone most of the time. He sometimes traveled down to the territory of Judah, even to Jerusalem, but most of the time his excursions were in Galilee around the lake. More than once he and his disciples had shipped off on the water. Indeed, that is how he departed soon before my daughter became ill.

I was not overly concerned when she became fatigued. She was twelve years old, soon to enter into womanhood. Perhaps she had already begun. I did not inquire into such female matters. My wife was in charge of that area. I was occupied with my duties at work.

I came home one day to find my daughter still in bed. She was feverous. My wife was anxious. I called for the physician. He prepared some kind of ointment for her and left. My wife and I stayed with her through the night. Her fever seemed to grow worse even as we tended her with wet cloths for her head. I called for the physician again. He stayed but seemed as powerless as I to curb the fever.

She tossed and turned in the bed, trying to get relief from the aches she felt all over. She was hot, then cold with chills, then hot again. I called for whatever physicians could be found. Two others came, but their efforts were just as useless, and it was clear as the night fell that she would die if her fever did not break.

The night—how long was the night! If I could only take her place, take her aches, her pain, her fever upon myself. Just do anything! But all I could do was hold her hand. Near the dawn came the greatest agony for myself. In her delirium she called my name. "Abba, help me. Abba, where are you? Abba, why have you left me?"

"I am here, my daughter! I have not left you." But she could not hear me. She was dying.

The sun rose. Someone had sent word for the mourners, and they settled in the main room, waiting for my daughter's death to begin their wailing. A servant stepped into the room and whispered in my ear, "He has returned."

"What? Who? Jesus? Where is he?" His boat had returned, and he was still at the lake's edge already besieged by the townspeople.

I rushed out of the house past the mourners. I must have looked like a fool running down the streets. I pushed through the crowd, calling out, "Teacher! Teacher!" Finally breaking through, I fell before his feet. "My daughter is dying. Come, save her."

He lifted me up. "Have faith. All will be well."

We started back to the house. The crowd! People, just get out of the way! Our pace was so slow because of the mob crowding around him. Jesus' disciples had to push them back to make a path. And then Jesus stops! He stops in the middle of the street and asks who touched him. Are you kidding me? Peter said what was in my mind: "The crowd is pressing on you and you ask who touched you?" Exactly! What was the Teacher doing?

But he persisted. Power had gone out of him. Oh no. We were likely already too late, and now Jesus feels his power being drained.

A trembling woman stepped forward and fell down before him, just as I had. She said something about an illness she had had for twelve years (the life of my daughter). Touching his garment had healed her. He spoke to her as if he had all the time in the world. He took her hand and lifted her up: "Daughter, your faith has made you well."

At that moment a friend came from my house. "Your daughter is dead; do not trouble the Teacher any more." I was too late. I was too late with help, and I wasn't even there for my daughter when she breathed her last breath. I had failed her.

I started to crumble to the ground when Jesus grabbed me. "Do not fear; only believe, and she will be well." I nodded numbly. We walked, this time with two of his disciples holding me up. We finally arrived and entered the house. The mourners were wailing and playing their music. My wife, also wailing loudly, fell into my arms. Then over the noise the Teacher's voice rose. "Why are you wailing and weeping? The girl is not dead. She is merely sleeping."

He told me and my wife to take him into the room. No one else was allowed in except Peter and two other disciples. He shut the door and walked over to my daughter's bed. Without pause, he took her by the hand and said, "Child, arise." Just like that. She opened her eyes and sat up in bed with a yawn. Then he directed us to get her some food, as though she had simply taken a long sleep.

But she had not been asleep. She had died. I had sat by her bed, holding her hand, helplessly watching her life ebb away. Helplessly, helplessly watching. And all he said was "arise."

What is this authority he possesses? I have heard the authority of his preaching. I have seen the authority to cast out evil spirits and to heal. But authority over death itself? I had once been proud of my own authority in the synagogue. How silly, how trivial it now rightly appears in the face of death. Better it is to throw pride away and kneel before the One of True Authority, who commands the dead to rise, and they do rise as though out of a sleep.

The Woman with the Discharge

And there was a woman who had had a discharge of blood for twelve years, and though she had spent all her living on physicians, she could not be healed by anyone. She came up behind him and touched the fringe of his garment, and immediately her discharge of blood ceased.

—Luke 8:43–44

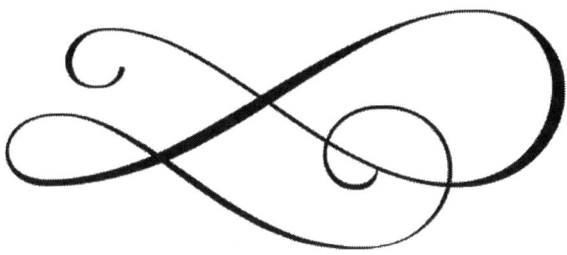

For Full Story:
Luke 8:43–48

My humiliation will soon end. Two more days before the final examination, then my offering of the two turtledoves, and it will be over. After twelve years I will live without shame, without the stigma of being avoided as one unclean. Perhaps I might finally be taken in marriage, if I am not considered too old.

I was betrothed when my condition began. My menstrual period had been heavier than usual. It lightened, but the flow continued. Surely it would end after a few days, I was told. Then weeks passed, months, and now years. Though weak, I did not feel ill. But, then, illness is not the trouble of such a problem. My discharge made me unclean. I was no better than a leper.

Everything I touched became unclean. No one could touch me; no one could sit or touch where I had been. I was barred from the women's court of the temple, from the temple grounds altogether. I was barred from the synagogue. My betrothal was broken. Who could marry a woman that could not be touched?

I tried everything, every doctor I could find. I swallowed their noxious potions and dishes which only made me nauseous. I followed their silly instructions that made me feel all the more foolish. And I paid for it all. I have nothing left. I had only what was left to me by my parents. I cannot earn a living. Who will buy what my hands have touched? I have been reduced to a leper's life.

Yes, I have prayed for healing. I prayed every day. I pleaded with God for mercy, for forgiveness. The priests told me that sin was the cause of my affliction. But what sin? I had not given my body to sin. I was faithful to my betrothed. I honored my parents. What had I done to deserve twelve years of such misery?

The Woman with the Discharge

News came of a man of God who was a healer. Everyone he touched was healed, and he turned no one away. It was said that he even cleansed lepers. Lepers! He was always traveling but would return to Capernaum, his home base. I thought of going there. It was not far.

But what will I do when I arrive? I am told that crowds are always around him. How can I get near? Stand in line? I would be shooed away. I would not be allowed near. How lepers got near, I do not know. Do I push myself forward? I am not bold. Oh, the humiliation of it all! The shame of having to tell of my condition in front of all those people.

But I have got to try. If Jesus can cleanse lepers, he can cleanse me. There must be healing power in him. Why should I believe in him, you ask, when the physicians have failed? Because he has actually healed! A touch of his hand has healed everyone. I know that if he touches me, I too will be healed. But the thought of pushing my way in front of him, to publicize my condition and shame before so many eyes—I have seen too many times the looks of fear and disgust by men, especially priests and religious leaders. Only the leper do they shun more fiercely than an unclean woman. No, I have not the courage to stand, even to kneel before this holy man.

If only I were bold. If only I were not so fearful. What can I do? If I cannot bear his touching me, I could touch him. There is power in him. There must be. But can the unclean touch what is holy? Will I not then contaminate him? Yet, he has touched lepers. I must try.

I arrive at the same time Jesus arrives by boat. Just as I have heard, he is surrounded by people. I pick up what little courage I have and begin to press through the crowd, when some man runs past me shouting. If only I had such boldness. His daughter is dying. Now the crowded really is excited. Another miracle to see. Jesus starts off with the man, but just to walk forward his disciples have to push people back. What am I to do now? How do I get past the disciples?

But he is coming my way. If I can keep my feet I will be close enough to touch his garment. No one need know, not even him. There are so many other hands touching him, how would my hand be noticed?

They are making their way by me. That father has him by the elbow on the other side. Their backs are to me. Now, just reach out. Touch the robe. That's it. What's happening? I feel a charge running through me! It worked! Praise the Blessed One on High!

But wait. Why has Jesus stopped? "Who touched my garments?" He is looking around.

A disciple replies, "You see the crowd pressing around you, and yet you say, 'Who touched me?'"

His eyes settle on me. "Power has gone from me." He looks straight at me. His disciples look at me. The father stares at me. All eyes turn to me.

There is no place to hide. I want to slink away. No, I don't. I have been healed. Jesus has healed me. I know it. Is he angry? I had no permission to touch him, no right to draw his power. Did I actually do that, draw power from him? He could feel power leave his body? I had no idea. It never occurred to me that he would feel anything.

I must admit what I have done. I fall before him. I tell him I am sorry for my boldness, and then the words flow. I tell all. I tell of my condition, the years, the shame, the misery. I weep for the pain and shame; I weep over the embarrassment I am feeling now.

I pause. Everyone is quiet. I look up into the face of Jesus. He smiles. "Daughter, your faith has made you well; go in peace, and be healed of your disease."

The father urges Jesus to move on. The crowd follows. I make my way back home.

He called me, "Daughter." That made me cry again. How many years has it been that someone addressed me affectionately? I don't quite know what he meant about my faith making me well. It was his power that healed me. Would it have not, if I had not believed it would? Could I have blunted it? I am not more powerful than Jesus.

Maybe it was the faith that led me to stretch out my hand, the faith that pushed me through my fear and shame to him. It is true that I would not have dared to force myself through that crowd if I had not believed in his power.

It was terrifying, but I am glad now that Jesus stopped and drew me out. Otherwise I would not have received his blessing. "Go in peace." I am at peace. At peace because I am healed. At peace because I know that Jesus is pleased with me. At peace knowing that the power drawn from him is given freely by him. I did not take what he was unaware of. I did not take what he was not willing to give gladly.

He said, "Be healed of your disease." I thought that was odd to say since I had already been healed. I see now that he meant fully healed. Healed in body but also in mind and spirit. The scars are healing.

Just two more days to reach the seventh day of my healing. On the eighth day I shall take the two turtledoves to the priest in the temple, one for a sin offering and the other for a burnt offering. He shall then make atonement for me before the Lord for my unclean discharge. Then, fully healed and fully at peace before my Lord, I will venture forth without fear.

The Boy with the Fish

One of his disciples, Andrew, Simon Peter's brother, said to him, "There is a boy here who has five barley loaves and two fish, but what are they for so many?" Jesus said, "Have the people sit down." Now there was much grass in the place. So the men sat down, about five thousand in number.

—John 6:8–10

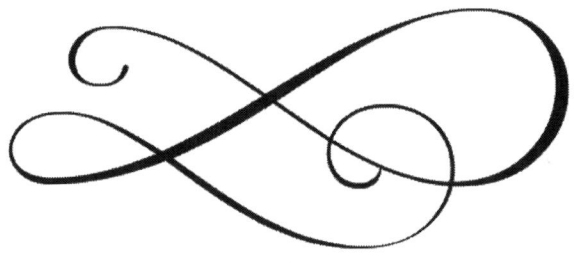

For full story:
John 6:1–14

The Teacher taught us to share. That's why I shared my food. He said we ought to do for others what we want for ourselves. If I was hungry, I would want someone to share food with me. He taught other things too. If I love God I will obey what he tells me to do. I can pray to God and ask him for things just as if he were my father. I shouldn't be calling other people names. Before I try to get a splinter out of someone else's eye, I should get the beam out of mine! That was funny.

I am with my parents. We are traveling up to Jerusalem to observe the Passover. We live just north of Bethsaida and have a long way to walk. But its fun. We are walking with lots of other families, and I have a lot of friends. It was just outside the village when we came across everybody listening to the Teacher. I heard my parents and neighbors talk about him, how he could heal anybody. They said that he even made the blind see!

We were all excited to see him. He was at the top of the hill looking out over the water. He must have already done all his healings because he was just teaching when we got close enough to listen. I was disappointed. I wanted to see miracles. But at least I was going to see him. My friends and I got permission to go up closer, and we took our lunches with us.

I'd never heard anybody like him before. I know I am just a boy, but the way the Teacher talked he was easy to listen to, even if I couldn't understand everything. I know he was talking to adults, but he would look at all of us, even us kids, when he was talking. I could tell that he didn't think we were a bother. I think he liked having us around.

There were some little children running around near him, and they didn't bother him at all. He even picked up a little girl, and he said that the grownups had to have the faith of a child like her. He really did!

The Boy with the Fish

It was getting late in the day. I saw some of his disciples were talking to each other like they were worried about something. One of them was waving his arm all around at the people. I crept closer to them.

"I told him that he needed to send the people away. It's getting late. Most of the people have no food."

"What did he tell you?"

"You feed them."

"What?"

"Even if we had the money to buy the food, where are we going to get it?"

That made me realize I had forgotten all about my lunch. I was so interested listening to the Teacher I had forgotten to be hungry! I felt it then. I was so glad to have something to eat. It wasn't much, but I liked it: two dried fish and five barley loaves.

And that's when the Teacher's words came back to me. If I didn't have food, I sure would want someone to share with me. I walked up to the one standing a little off from the others. I liked his face. He was the one disciple that looked over at us boys and even smiled.

"Sir, I'd like to share my food."

He looked at me with surprise and then smiled.

"Come, lad. Let me take you to the Teacher."

I was nervous. I thought the man, if he didn't laugh at me, would just take the food himself to the Teacher. He told me his name was Andrew. He made me feel comfortable and said that Jesus—that's the name of the Teacher—would want to meet me.

We walked up to Jesus. A couple of other disciples were talking to him about the problem of food. I could tell they were frustrated, but he didn't seemed troubled at all. Andrew spoke, "There is a boy here who has five barley loaves and two fish." The other disciples looked at him and then me like we were crazy. We both felt foolish. I guess that's why Andrew added, "but what are they for so many?"

But the Teacher acted as if that was the most natural thing in the world what we offered. I think he was even waiting for me or someone to come with food. He didn't laugh at me, and he didn't frown at Andrew. He didn't even scold the other disciples. He acted like everything was going just as he had planned.

He had the disciples go around and have the people seated. Some of the people had already started to leave. He then had other disciples bring baskets. Then he took my barley loaves, said a blessing over them, and then placed each loaf in a basket. He did the same thing with the two fish—one in each basket.

That was so weird. I was thinking that he might thank me for sharing, that's all. Maybe he would encourage the people to share their food like me. What was putting each piece of bread and fish in baskets going to do?

Andrew told me to head back down. My friends had already joined their family, so I went over to my parents. I told them what I had done, and they were very proud of me. My mother still had a little food left and was bringing it out when we heard a commotion. We looked back up toward the Teacher and his disciples. They were now walking among the people with the baskets. They had more baskets than the ones I saw, and they seemed full. They were giving out food.

Did more people bring food like me? I was feeling good now about sharing. But how did so many people share so much food so quickly? I had just left the hilltop. Soon, two of the disciples came to us. Andrew was one of them, and he had a huge smile on his face. He showed me his basket full of fish. Now here is the strange part. It was the same fish I had brought to him!

There were not different types of fish. They were all the same size, the same dried small fish that I had. How could that be? And the basket of loaves. They were all the same small barley loaves that I had shared. These were my fish and bread! I know I am just a boy, but I promise you I am telling the truth. Jesus, the Teacher, did a miracle. He multiplied the food I had shared. He did a miracle, and I got to see it! He used my fish, my bread.

Andrew walked on laughing. My parents wanted to know what was so funny. At first they frowned and were about to correct me, but my mother examined the fish and the bread. She knew they were the same she had given me. It wasn't long before everyone realized that a miracle had been performed.

Who has ever seen anything like this? This is like the manna that came to our ancestors in the wilderness. No, it was even greater. Who can make a little fish and bread multiply so that they feed thousands of people?

People started talking among themselves. "This is the Prophet who is to come." Everyone was excited now. I heard others yell out, "Blessed is he who comes in the name of the Lord!" And "Hosanna to the Son of David!"

I don't know what all happened after that. I wanted to stay, but my parents pulled me away. It was starting to get dark, and they wanted to find a place to spend the night. We still have a long journey to Jerusalem.

But I cannot sleep. Not after what I have seen. And to think, Jesus—they call him Jesus of Nazareth—used me, even a boy, even with the little that I had. I didn't know he was going to do a miracle with my fish and bread. All I knew was that he wanted me to share what I had. He just wanted me to give. It might only be a little but he could turn it into a lot.

Peter on the Water

And in the fourth watch of the night he came to them, walking on the sea. But when the disciples saw him walking on the sea, they were terrified, and said, "It is a ghost!" and they cried out in fear. But immediately Jesus spoke to them, saying, "Take heart; it is I. Do not be afraid."

—Matthew 14:25–27

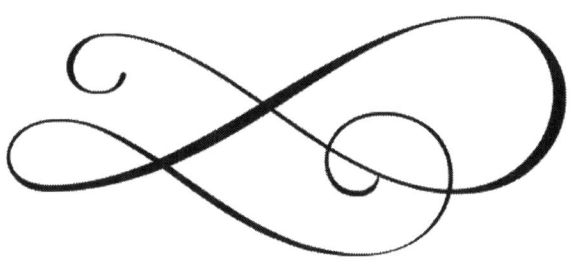

For full story:
Matthew 14:22–33

Little faith. "You of little faith," is what he called me as he lifted me out of the water.

After feeding the great crowd, Jesus wanted to be alone. He did not like their reaction to the miracle feeding. Their exuberance was growing. Some began hailing him as prophet, others even the Messiah. They were ready then and there to make him king. And so he ordered us to disperse the crowd. He wanted us to then cast off in the boat for the other side of the lake, while he slipped away up into the mountain to pray.

We were confused. Had he not come for the purpose of ascending to the throne? Perhaps it was not time. But why send us away? How was he to join us? But we did not question him. There were times when he had a determined look that told us not to question.

So we got into the boat and cast off. The journey was difficult from the start as the wind was against us. We could not use the sail but had to row. We were at it for what seemed like hours, for the wind only grew stronger so that waves were beating against the prow. Exhaustion had set in all of us, though we took turns rowing to keep up our strength. We fishermen took the brunt of the work. We had to if we were to make headway.

The night sky was clear with a nearly full moon. We could just make out hills where we were heading. All our rowing had only taken us three or four miles, but we needed to be patient and row steadily. But what about our Master, Jesus? How did he plan to meet up with us? Perhaps he has arranged for a boat. Perhaps he will walk. He will make just as good time as we against this wind.

Stroke, stroke. And then an alarming cry. "It is a ghost!" shouted one of the men. The strain, the lack of sleep, the tricks the night on water can play, no doubt were playing with his mind. But others joined in pointing over the water from where we had just been. They were seeing something. We all peered at the spot. It was true. Someone, some thing, was moving across the water, like a man walking, walking as though on solid ground.

We are not normally superstitious men, but how could we account for all seeing the same apparition, if it were not real? It began to walk past us. Now we were all crying out in alarm.

And then he called out, "Take heart; it is I. Do not be afraid."

It was Jesus, our Master! We were all filled with wonder, a terrified wonder. Jesus is walking on the water, on the sea with its waves crashing about, with the wind howling. He was walking without effort as if all was calm about him.

He was not far, no more than a few yards. I was looking at him, fixed on his eyes. I felt that he was looking straight at me. I felt a thrill in my heart. There was nothing, nothing that this man could not do. He had commanded the storm and waves before. I knew then that he was more than a man. He must even now have commanded the sea to bear his feet and the wind to go around him. Whatever he commands must obey him. Whatever he commands. "Lord, if it is you, (and I knew without doubt it was my Lord) command me to come to you on the water."

"Come."

Every fiber of my being felt the thrill of that command. My eyes never left his as I stepped over the side and planted my feet on hard surface. I did not hesitate. I walked toward him as if in a dream. And then I felt the splash of water on my skin. I blinked. The wind was blowing in my face. I heard its howling. I looked about me at the waves. The boat was moving away. I looked down and saw my feet under water. I was sinking! I was drowning!

"Lord, save me! Save me!"

I felt a strong hand grip mine. He pulled me up as a man pulls up a little child who has fallen down in a puddle. He pulled me up and set my feet on solid water. With his arm around me we walked to the boat and climbed in.

As I caught my breath, I became aware that the wind had ceased. All was calm. I turned to Jesus. That's when he said, "O you of little faith, why did you doubt?"

Even now I'm not sure the tone of his voice. Was he frowning or smiling? There was a great commotion in the boat as my brothers dropped on their knees. "Truly you are the Son of God!" they cried out in worship.

But it was his words to me that preoccupied my mind. Of little faith. Was it little faith that recognized his power to command me to walk on the water? Was it little faith that moved me to step out of the boat? My brothers worshiping next to me and exclaiming with an exalted faith—none of them had stepped out of the boat with me.

I obeyed my Lord's command. I walked on the water! I walked toward my Lord my eyes fixed on him. I walked with faith, great faith.

Until…until I felt the spray of the water, heard the howling of the wind, looked at the hurling waves…until I looked away from Jesus, the one who commanded me to come to him.

"Why did you doubt?" he asked.

It was easy to explain. I was sinking. I was going under. The storm about me was pushing me down below the waves. Is that not enough reason to doubt I could stay up? That I would be safe without his intervention? I did not doubt my Lord's ability to save me. That is why I cried out to him. And I had no doubt that I would remain safe while his arm was around me, that I would not sink again.

But Jesus wanted to know about the doubt that led me to sink in the first place. If faith compelled me to step over the side of the boat, and faith kept me up as I walked toward Jesus, what happened that led to my sinking? How did doubt slip in and push away the faith?

Yes, why the doubt? What happened to me? I remember now. I had been transfixed on Jesus. And while my eyes were riveted on his, the storm about me faded into the background. I had eyes for nothing else but Jesus. And when he had spoken to me, when he had commanded, "Come," I heard nothing else. There was no howling wind, no raging waters. There was not a boat with other men. There was only Jesus with his eyes on me, beckoning me to him.

But I could not maintain the fixation. The water was real, and it was not long before I felt the wetness of the spray. That sensation startled me, and it was then that the wind returned to reality, and the night and what seemed a vast sea. I turned my eyes from Jesus, from his commanding presence, from his eyes that had remained fixed on mine. The power of my surroundings became greater reality than the power of his presence.

I doubted because I blinked, because my blink shifted my eyes away from my Lord and to my fears. I know no greater fear than drowning, yes, me the fisherman. I fear it. I have nightmares about it. To sink and sink with no hope of rising again. Even now the idea shakes me.

I remember as a child hearing the story of Jonah read and how it terrified me. I can recall the words of the prophet:

> The waters closed in over me to take my life;
>   the deep surrounded me;
> weeds were wrapped about my head
>   at the roots of the mountains.
> I went down to the land
>   whose bars closed upon me forever.

I doubted because I feared. It's as plain as that. Do you ever have such fear? Is there nothing that does not make you tremble just to think of it?

Even though I doubted I had enough wits about me, still enough faith, as small as it may be, to call out to my Lord. And he did not let me down, did not let me sink down. He pulled me up. I may not have perfect faith. I may not have overcome all my fears. But one thing I know: my Lord will deliver me when I call upon him. Out of my distress, he will answer me.

The Canaanite Woman

And Jesus went away from there and withdrew to the district of Tyre and Sidon. And behold, a Canaanite woman from that region came out and was crying, "Have mercy on me, O Lord, Son of David; my daughter is severely oppressed by a demon." But he did not answer her a word.

—Matthew 15:21–23

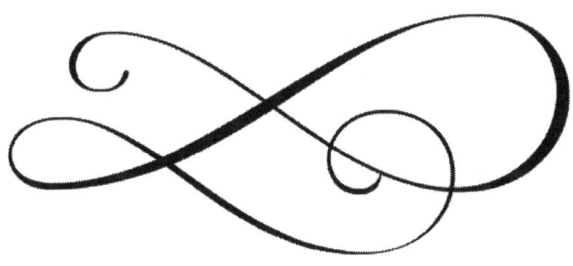

For Full Story:
Matthew 15:21–28

N

o, I was not offended, nor was I surprised by his remark. I knew what to expect because I understood who Jesus was, at least I thought I did. If I had really known, then I might have been surprised.

I live in the Syro-Phoenicia district of Syria, just above Galilee where Jesus was operating. Yes, I knew who he was. Everyone was talking about him. They called him Prophet, Man of God, Teacher, but there were those who even spoke of him as the Son of David, the Messiah.

The Jews are always talking about their Messiah who is going to redeem them from their hated oppressors, the Romans. I do not find life under the Roman Empire particularly oppressive. Their rule, if anything, moderates the unjust practices of our local rulers. But the Jews hate the idea of being subjected to anyone. They are God's covenant people, better than anyone else. They are so arrogant and so stubborn that even their Roman rulers avoid offending them when possible. Why, I have heard that the Roman procurator will even come out of his house to speak with their leaders, so that they will not be made unclean. And don't even dare enter their homes. All Gentiles are unclean, and Jews—especially Jewish religious leaders—cannot be dirtied by contact with us. Imagine their horror if a Gentile entered into their home.

That is why I knew what to expect when I committed the sacrilegious act of entering the habitation of a Jewish holy man. But I am above all a mother, and my daughter was in anguish, oppressed by a demon. When I heard that Jesus was nearby, I had to go. Whatever else may be true of him, one thing I did know—that he was a miracle worker. The stories had poured in of how he healed everyone—everyone! Those who were sick—even blind—and those who were plagued by demons. Yes, he was driving out demons. They could not withstand him.

But all of these miracles were for his people, not outsiders. I knew he was hiding out. I knew he would not want visitors and definitely not a Gentile. I knew I would likely face rejection, but my daughter was suffering, and I would not be denied.

I found where he was staying, walked straight in, and cried out to him, "Have mercy on me, O Lord, Son of David; my daughter is severely oppressed by a demon!" There was silence. I had surprised the teacher and his men. Those men! The surprise and then the disgust were clear on their faces. They looked to their master, who made no reply. He looked at me with a face I could not read. There was not the same disgust, but…what was it? Then he turned his back and walked away.

His disciples tried to escort me out of the door, but I shook off their hands and cried out all the louder. They blocked my way to Jesus, but all the more I called out. I didn't care what they thought of me. They would have to drag me out of that house, and if they had, I would have barged back in. My daughter was suffering, and here was the man who could heal her. No one was going to stop me from getting to him and getting through to him.

Finally he spoke. "I was sent only to the lost sheep of the house of Israel." Not the answer I wanted, but one that I expected. I had no claim on him. He had no obligation to me. I was the outsider, as was plain to all in that house. There was no pity.

The men looked at me sternly and with the expectation that I would now turn away. But I rushed through them and fell before the man of God. "Lord, help me." I don't know why I acted as I did. It was clear that I could expect no help, and yet, I somehow knew that if he would, he had the power to heal my daughter. Perhaps I spoke out of sheer desperation. All I know was that he was my last chance, and I could not leave without him.

"It is not right to take the children's bread and throw it to the dogs." Those are the words that have shocked everyone who has heard my story. I think even his callous disciples winced at that remark. I am on my knees pleading for mercy, and my helper insults me and my daughter.

Oddly enough, it was that insult that brought back my wits. Like I said, I had known what to expect. I had known that I was likely to be refused. But when he gave the first rebuttal, I had given way to emotion. The comment about dogs—I had heard that insult before from Jews who regarded all of us Gentiles as beneath them. If I were going to get through to this Jewish teacher, it had to be by wit and not by emotion.

"Yes, Lord, yet even the dogs eat the crumbs that fall from their masters' table." Complete silence. The men in the room were astonished. They looked to their master for his reply. They and I wondered what he would do. Did I push too far? Would he throw me out?

He smiled. His somber face broke into a big smile! "O woman, great is your faith! Be it done for you as you desire."

"Great is your faith." I suppose I did have strong faith. I had not thought about it. All I had known was that this was the man who could heal my daughter, and I intended not to be denied. He was a man of God, even thought by some to be the Son of David, the Messiah for the Jews. Perhaps he was. Whoever he was precisely, his miracles of healing and driving out demons proved at least that he had God behind him. For all my resentment of the Jews' feelings of superiority, I could not deny the power of their religion and the uniqueness of their God: no idols, no collection of gods, just faith in this one, all-supreme Lord God. He was a god to be reckoned with, and this Jesus of Nazareth, this Son of David, was clearly a man of God to be reckoned with. That is what I knew. That, I suppose, was the faith that made me determined.

And that was the faith that helped me to believe he had answered my plea. My daughter was still at home. I had intended to plead for him to come with me. Yet, he spoke simply, confidently, as though he were giving an order. "Be it done." I could not but believe that it was done, that I would find my daughter healed, her demon gone.

I looked at Jesus again with his smile. He certainly was happy; he even seemed proud...of me! I had broken into the house as an outcast; I walked out as though the star pupil of a teacher's class. Or, rather, I rushed out, for I had a daughter—a healed daughter—to see. I found her, just as he indicated—healed and in her right mind. We sat on the bed, her head on my shoulder.

Faith can be a funny thing. I had not known the faith inside me until its object had drawn near. However strong my faith might be, I knew that what mattered was the person in whom I placed that faith. I would not be denied seeing him; I would not be denied pleading with him; and he would not be denied the order he gave, even as he smiled.

The Half-Believing Father

And when they came to the disciples, they saw a great crowd around them, and scribes arguing with them. And immediately all the crowd, when they saw him, were greatly amazed and ran up to him and greeted him. And he asked them, "What are you arguing about with them?" And someone from the crowd answered him, "Teacher, I brought my son to you…"

—Mark 9:14–17

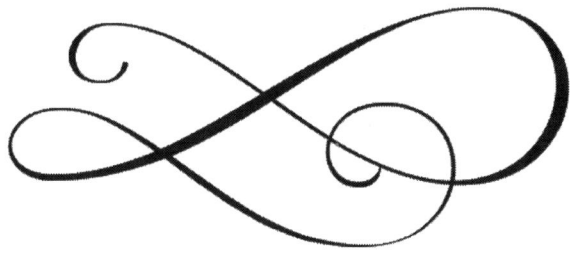

For full story:
Mark 9:14–27

It just came out. I had not intended to say it, or rather, to admit it. I had the whole speech planned from the time I first set out with my son to see the Teacher. That's how everyone referred to him, though word was getting around that he might be more—perhaps the Anointed One. His teaching was accompanied with miracle working power, and that is why I traveled to see him with my son.

From early on he has suffered from seizures that wrack his body so horribly he falls to the ground writhing and foaming at the mouth. I believe a spirit possessed him, desiring to kill him. Why else did his seizures happen so often around fire or water, so that he came close to burning himself or drowning? Perhaps it was the result of successive seizures that my son became mute. His only sounds were those of anguish moans and even shrieks.

The heartache of a father lies not only in watching his son suffer but in not being able to do anything about it other than to try and protect him in his agonies. And there are the interim times between the seizures that in themselves are burdens, for no one knows when the next affliction will occur. Next week? Next month? Tomorrow? Today? His mute condition is an ever-present reminder that he is not healed.

I hear about the Teacher, a power-working prophet who heals everyone who comes to him, whatever the illness. Why, they say that he even cleanses lepers! If he will help such outcasts, surely he would have compassion on my boy.

I thought everything through. I would lead my son to him, pay him due honor, then introduce my son with the appeal toward his pity. If he could do it—and everyone said he could—then my son would be healed. I was certain of it, if what everyone said was true. It must be true. I was told he had cast out spirits, and that is what my son had—an evil spirit. Yes, it was going to all work out. The Teacher would take pity on my boy and heal him.

The Half-Believing Father

It was at least worth a try. I had tried everything else—doctors, potions, other so-called healers. This man seemed to be the real deal. He must be capable. Years of failure, though, and I can't but have a little doubt that this would be the end of my son's sufferings. But I didn't doubt. No, no, I would take my son to the Teacher, say the right words, and he would heal my son.

So I go. I travel to the town where he is supposed to be, and he is not there! Just my luck. But, the Teacher's disciples are there, and they assure me that they can heal my son. They had done the same thing themselves. Jesus, the Teacher, had sent them out before, and they had healed and cast out evil spirits.

"Good, go for it," I said. So one came up, turned to my son, and cried out, "Come forth, evil spirit!" My son looked over at me with a quizzical look. Another of the disciples stepped up: "Come forth in the name of Jesus!" My son yawned, but no visible change. And so they all took their turn, changing the words a bit. "Come out"; "leave"; "come out mute spirit"; "come out epileptic spirit"; "please come out."

"This can't get worse," I thought. And then it did. I began to notice others. A crowd was gathering. My son does not like crowds, and neither of us like having lots a people stare at us. Then someone spoke up. "You cannot drive out evil spirits because you follow a false teacher." "Yes," another one added, "and your teacher is conveniently absent when a real affliction is presented." They were scribes—teachers of the law. They doubted Jesus. Indeed, they outright accused him of being a fake. An argument ensued, and my son and I stepped to the side.

Maybe all of this was but another failed effort. Maybe this Jesus of Nazareth was not... Then another voice broke forth—a clear, commanding voice. "What are you arguing about with them?" It was the Teacher! This was my chance! I broke through to him.

"Teacher, I brought my son to you, for he has a spirit that makes him mute. And whenever it seizes him, it throws him down, and he foams and grinds his teeth and becomes rigid. So I asked your disciples to cast it out, and they were not able." There, I got it out, almost as I had rehearsed. The failure of his disciples and the embarrassing debate had rattled me. I forgot

155

to appeal to his compassion. I didn't even ask Jesus to do anything. And his response did not indicate he was feeling much pity—"O faithless generation, how long am I to bear with you?"

But then hope again: "Bring him to me." Now is when it gets fuzzy for me. I bring my son in front and the seizure begins. He falls onto the ground in convulsions, foaming at the mouth. My heart is wrenched. I've seen this so many times, feeling helpless as ever. But now the Teacher is here. Surely he will do something.

But instead he asks me a question—how long my son had had these seizures. What? Did it matter? No one told me I would be questioned. Why for my son? Why now? Is something wrong? Is he hesitating?

I tell him. "From childhood. And it has often cast him into fire and water, to destroy him." I had forgotten to tell him that—a key detail to draw out his pity! But he looks unmoved. Does he lack pity still? Or does he lack power? My son's convulsions grow worse. "But if you can do anything, have compassion on us and help us," I plead.

Will there now be a miracle? I look at my son and then at the Teacher. Surely he sees my anguish; surely he must have pity. If he can only help. And then he horrifies me. "If you can! All things are possible for one who believes." The compassionate Teacher has turned on me. What have I done? I'm the one who has brought my son to Jesus. And now, because I don't get the formula right—I slip up and use the taboo word "if"—he becomes incensed? All right, "I do believe!"

We look at each other straight in the eyes, and we both know I don't believe. The doubt had been in my heart even as I began the journey with my son. I had come to Jesus out of desperation, wanting to believe, doing my best to convince myself that this would not turn out to be yet another false trail to my son's healing. I had prepared to say the right words, to follow the script so that, if this Teacher was the real deal, he would then do the healing. Then not finding him; then the failure of his disciples; then the crowd gathering and the scribes arguing—nothing is going according to plan, especially when the Teacher shows up, especially now.

And so I tell the truth, what really is in my heart, and I ask for help, not for my son but for me. "Help me in my unbelief!" Help *me*! Help me with my doubt born from fruitless attempts to help my son. Help me put down my mask of self-confidence, of depending upon my own ability to say the right words, to do the right things to prove myself a good man. Help me with whatever it is I need in my weakness.

The Teacher does not respond to me. He looks around at his defeated disciples, at the smirking scribes, and the crowd enjoying the entertainment. Then he calls out the spirit; no, he orders the spirit to come out as a master gives orders to a slave. And the spirit comes out as though it is possessed, as though it is terrified of Jesus. It wracks my son violently one more time and then leaves him for dead. But he isn't. The Teacher stoops down, takes my son's hand, and lifts him up as though out of a deep sleep. And for the first time in too many years, my son says to me, "Father."

The Teacher healed my son, not when I expressed the faith he valued so highly but when I admitted the little faith I possessed, or was it because I asked help for my unbelief? The Teacher needed nothing from me and yet demanded much from me. I gave him nothing and asked help for myself. And my son was healed. We journeyed back home healed—son and father. My son talked nonstop. It was I who was mute in contemplation.

The Man Born Blind

As he passed by, he saw a man blind from birth. And his disciples asked him, "Rabbi, who sinned, this man or his parents, that he was born blind?" Jesus answered, "It was not that this man sinned, or his parents, but that the works of God might be displayed in him."

—John 9:1–3

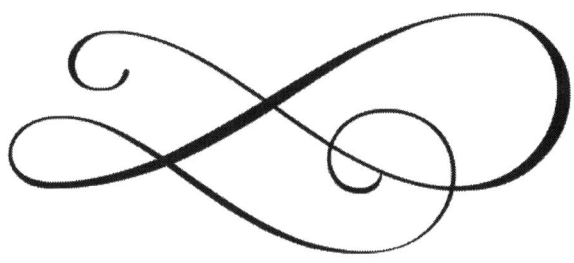

For full story:
John 9:1–41

Why would they not believe? Why the hardness of spirit? Why the blindness?

I was born blind. People said it was God's punishment. For what? What sin had I committed in the womb other than to make my mother queasy and her ribs soar from kicking? Some said it was for my parents' sins. I cannot deny they were sinners, but then who can claim to be without sin? My mother loved me; my father was kind enough for a man shamed by a blind son. I've had no complaints.

They were poor, and I was of no help to them other than to earn coins by begging. My parents would take me to the temple stairs to beg from passersby entering or leaving the temple. Because almsgiving was regarded as a means of earning merit before God, I could rely on a steady stream of income. I became rather good at the system over the years, learning the best times of the day and the best days of the year and the best locations. Feast days and Sabbath days are good, as worshipers feel all the more compelled to give to the poor.

Over time I even built up a clientele, so to speak. I could recognize voices, even footsteps, and greet my benefactors by name. I did not recognize, though, the footsteps that stopped in front of me one Sabbath day. I knew someone was staring at me.

"Help a poor man born blind!" I cried out. But there was no answer.

Then a voice off to the side: "Rabbi, who sinned, this man or his parents, that he was born blind?"

So that was what this was about—some new religious teacher with his little group of disciples. A Pharisee, no doubt. I had had this experience before—being the object lesson for a theological discussion. It goes with the territory of sitting near the temple where these rabbis gather with their pupils. What is particularly galling is that no one ever speaks to me. It is as if I am deaf as well as blind to them.

But this rabbi gave an answer no other teacher had given. "It was not that this man sinned, or his parents."

That perked up my ears and even more what he said next. "But that the works of God might be displayed in him."

I heard him spit. He was right next to me, and I could tell he had knelt down. The next thing I knew he was placing mud over my eyes. I didn't move. From the authority of his voice, I knew this was a man to take seriously. He took my hands and stood me up, then gave the command to go wash my eyes in the pool of Siloam.

And I went. Just like that. I don't really know why other than to say that his voice was one to be obeyed. The pool was a few minutes' walk away. You might wonder how I could have gotten there, but one advantage of being born blind is that you learn how to get around on your own, and I knew the streets and lanes of Jerusalem as well as any seeing man. I came to the pool, bent down, and began washing my eyes and face.

Something painful was piercing my eyes. Where there had always been a cool darkness, now, what I came to understand was light was hitting my eyes and making me dizzy. I...could see! How strange it was! There were images but I did not know how to recognize them. And I was first seeing things through the reflection of the water, making everything even stranger.

I closed my eyes, steadied myself, and slowly opened them again. Fuzzy images began to take shape and become clearer. Even so, where before I could walk anywhere easily, I now began to stretch out my hands and call for help to walk. Someone came over.

"I can see!" I exclaimed, and then stumbled into his arms.

"You are drunk," he replied.

"No, I see you and that bird—it must be a bird—which is flying. That moving light over there must be the pool. And that creature with the hump—is that a camel? I can see! Take me back to the Rabbi Jesus now!"

He held my arm as we walked back to the temple and answered all my questions. "That's a donkey." "That's the color blue and that is red." "Yes, there are many kinds of colors; you are wearing brown."

People who recognized me begging on the streets joined us. Even some neighbors saw me. They could not believe their eyes. They all wanted to know what had happened. I told them about Jesus, but when we returned to the spot where he had touched me, he was gone. Before I knew it, the people around me had taken me by the arms to see the Pharisees. They needed some religious authority to account for what had happened.

The Pharisees questioned me, and I told them about Jesus healing me. I expected them to be amazed like my neighbors and to want to find Jesus. Instead, they reacted with anger, and then they started their same old theological debates about who sinned. It was a Sabbath day, and that is what bothered them. God forbid that a man born blind be healed on the Sabbath day! This Jesus must be a sinner.

They asked me what I thought, and I evidently gave the wrong answer: "He is a prophet." It seemed a simple equation. I was born blind. Born blind, mind you. Jesus, already acknowledged a rabbi, healed me. If I recall the Scriptures correctly, that's the kind of stuff prophets did.

You could tell they were in a quandary as to what to do. I should have known what they would come up with. They accused me of being a liar—not about Jesus, but about me! They claimed I had not been blind. Evidently I had been faking it all these years. They wanted proof, and so they sent for my parents. That only made it worse for them.

So after my dear parents confirmed that I had been blind, the Pharisees turned to me again with the nerve to say, "Give glory to God."

That is what I had been trying to do! Jesus had said that I had been born blind for that very purpose. My healing displayed the mighty works of God. How difficult can this be? But they were hung up on this a-man-of-God-wouldn't-break-the-Sabbath bit, and they just would not believe. And then I began to understand that they had already known about this Jesus and had hardened against him. He did not follow the party line.

Funny how it is in encountering skepticism that the truth becomes so clear, as clear as light entering into a blind man's eyes. I admonished them: "You do not know where he comes from, and yet he opened my eyes. We know that God does not listen to sinners, but if anyone is a worshiper of God and does his will, God listens to him. Never since the world began has it been heard that anyone opened the eyes of a man born blind. If this man were not from God, he could do nothing."

And so they kicked me out. What else could they do?

Then Jesus found me. How odd. When I was blind, I did not seek him nor asked to be healed. He came to me and healed me. When I tried to find him again, he was gone. But when I was cast out by my own religious leaders, then he found me again. When he revealed who he was, I did what I so eagerly wanted to do—I worshiped him.

It seemed strange that to heal me, Jesus would send me away from himself and not even remain to see my healing. I had to obey his odd command to leave, and I had to testify for him before the skeptical authorities alone. But I did obey and I did testify faithfully to his work. And in the end, he found me. He healed my blindness, first physically and then spiritually. Yes, spiritually. Is that not what the healing was really about? Jesus said in reaction to the Pharisees: "For judgment I came into this world, that those who do not see may see, and those who see may become blind." I have had enough of darkness now that the light has come.

Martha

Now as they went on their way, Jesus entered a village. And a woman named Martha welcomed him into her house. And she had a sister called Mary, who sat at the Lord's feet and listened to his teaching. But Martha was distracted …

—Luke 10:38–40

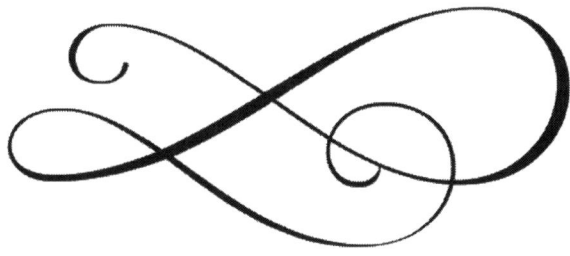

For full story:
Luke 10:38–42

Anxious and troubled about many things? I was put out that day, put out with my younger sister for her heedlessness. It is good and well to speak of Mary choosing the good portion, but all that did was to place on my shoulders all the responsibility for the not-so-good portion. Someone had to feed the crowd. Someone had to fulfill the role of hospitality. Is that not a trait valued by God?

It surely is a responsibility insisted upon in our culture. Was our Father Abraham criticized for feeding the three visitors? I had more than twenty, what with Jesus and his disciples, not to mention a few neighbors.

Don't get me wrong. I was pleased that Jesus would come into our home. I personally welcomed him, and I was fine with our brother Lazarus acting as host. That is his place as the oldest male. Our parents are deceased. I did not resent his sitting down with the Teacher and his disciples. That is appropriate for the men. They are the spiritual leaders. It is their place to sit at the feet of rabbis, study the Scriptures, and debate the law.

I don't even have a problem with women learning a bit or two. I would have been okay with Mary listening in *as we got our work done.* A meal had to be prepared! It is that simple. I don't need to be lectured. I know the law as well as most men, I dare say. "Man does not live by bread alone, but man lives by every word that comes from the mouth of the Lord." I know what Moses said. By bread *alone.* Man still needs bread. He also cannot live by words alone, even the words that come from the good Master.

Is that so hard to understand? It should not have been for Mary. Our mother raised us right. She taught us to cook, to sew, to do all that is needed to keep a home. We have servants, to be sure, but it is our responsibility—we, the women of this house—to keep up the good reputation of our house, as passed on from our parents. There are expectations to meet.

Mary has always understood this. I have had no complaints about her keeping up her portion of the work. Not until then; not until Jesus came into our home. I am not blaming him. He came in at our invitation, and he merely carried out his role as a rabbi—he taught. That is what teachers do. Lazarus played host. That is what he is supposed to do. All would have been fine if Mary had done what she was supposed to do—help prepare the meal. If time was left, she could stand outside the group and listen in.

That is another thing that, I admit, got under my skin. Where was Mary? Sitting at the Lord's feet! What was she thinking—that she was just another disciple? Did she suddenly not know what is and is not appropriate? She was sitting among men. She was nearly touching them, in our house! Again, what was she thinking? Not about the honor of her brother; not about me, that's for sure.

What was she thinking? I looked at her. She was looking at the Teacher, and it was clear that she was listening intently to him. What was he saying? I can't remember; I was too busy. That's the point—I was made too busy because she was listening to him. She had forgotten me. But surely the Master could see my distress. More than once I saw him glancing at me as I scurried about.

Finally, I had enough. "Lord, do you not care that my sister has left me to serve alone? Tell her then to help me." I cringe now at what I said. My mother would have been ashamed. My father—I don't want to think of his reaction. It was the height of rudeness even to speak up, but to rebuke our honored guest (yes, it was a rebuke) was inexcusable. If only Mary…

I am kidding myself—blaming my sister because she was actually listening to the Teacher. What was Mary thinking? The real question is what I was thinking. I am the older of the sisters. I should have known better. We do have servants, and I could have turned most of the work over to them. It was my pride. I didn't realize it then, but I do now. I did not appreciate his rebuke of me, to be sure, but I have not forgotten his words.

I ask about what Mary was thinking. The problem for me was that I was doing too much thinking. Not about what needed to be done for Jesus' comfort, nor for my brother's honor. My thoughts were all about me. What mattered to me was how I would be thought of, and I wanted to be thought of as the perfect hostess. I wanted everything just right so that I would be thought of like, well, I am a bit embarrassed to admit, as the excellent wife of Proverbs.

> Many women have done excellently,
> but you surpass them all.

God has not granted that I should be a wife, and I know that my time has passed to expect a husband. Still, I am the woman of the house, and I have a brother to care for until he should be married. What then, I don't know. Lazarus will keep his sisters in his home; I do not worry about that. But what will be my place, then? Where will my value lie when another woman takes my place?

"One thing is necessary." What did Jesus mean? One thing…one thing. Mary had chosen the better portion. What was that portion? It must have been listening to the Lord. That is what Mary was doing—listening, feeding upon his words, drinking them in, letting them nourish her, listening with understanding.

I did not do much listening that night. I still had a meal to complete and serve. I was not so much anxious as annoyed—annoyed with Jesus, as well as Mary, annoyed that I was rebuked in front of my guests, my brother, and especially my sister. What did everyone think of me? Lazarus had to be ashamed, though he has not mentioned the episode to me.

I did listen the next day before Jesus continued his journey. I have even listened to my sister this evening, what she had learned from the Teacher. Mary knows Jesus to be more than a teacher, even more than a prophet. She believes Jesus of Nazareth is the Messiah, the Son of God come into the world. The Messiah? How does she know? I have listened to the Teacher, and to be honest, the stories he tells confuse me, rather than make things clearer.

Jesus said that Mary had chosen the better portion. As I now take time to understand my sister better, I perceive that Mary not only listens, but she somehow has the ears that we others do not. I think she understands more than even Jesus' disciples. Why is that?

I think it goes back to thinking. As I have admitted, that night I was thinking about myself. Mary, I don't think she was thinking about herself at all. I saw the way she looked at the Teacher. All her thoughts were directed toward what he was saying. She was not thinking about how she appeared, whether to Jesus or to the disciples or to her brother or to me. She was simply listening. And when the two of us were together, and she talked to me about what she had been learning, even then she did not share her feelings. She certainly did not talk like other women about how she felt about Jesus or how she hoped he felt about her. She did not talk about the other men. She only spoke of what she heard, then perceived, then believed. May the Lord grant to me the will to choose this better portion.

The Lawyer

And behold, a lawyer stood up to put him to the test,
saying, "Teacher, what shall I do to inherit eternal life?"

—Luke 10:25

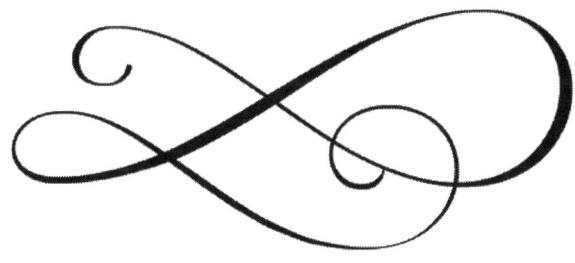

For full story:
Luke 10:25–37

I walked right into his trap. Mind you, I was not trying to trap Jesus. Test him, yes. That is what we lawyers and rabbis do to one another. We test each other's knowledge of the Law, of the Scriptures. That is how we sharpen one another, and that is how we root out the unorthodox. We ask questions.

And so, I asked a question: "What shall I do to inherit eternal life?" Of course, I knew the answer. I asked in this way because I wanted to see how this Teacher would answer, not a scholar of the Law, but a common sincere Jew.

Jesus pulled a classic move by turning the question back onto me: "What is written in the Law? How do you read it?" He refused to take my question any other way than what it really was—a scholarly discussion, and so I had to give an answer. "You shall love the Lord your God with all your heart and with all your soul and with all your strength and with all your mind, and your neighbor as yourself."

That, of course, is the orthodox answer, as it sums up the law. And Jesus acknowledged it as such.

"You have answered correctly; do this, and you will live."

There was nothing more to be said, and I ought to have left it at that. But then, I am a lawyer, a student of the holy Law. I could not let matters rest. Just who did Jesus include in that term of neighbor?

I had given thought to who "neighbor" entailed. Indeed, that was a common matter of debate. That phrase I quoted—"and your neighbor as yourself"—it comes from Moses' book of Leviticus. I can quote the full context.

> You shall not hate your brother in your heart, but you shall reason frankly with your neighbor, lest you incur sin because of him. You shall not take vengeance or bear a grudge against the sons of your own people, but you shall love your neighbor as yourself: I am the Lord.

It is clear that neighbor is equated with "sons of your own people." Does that not leave out foreigners? How else could it be read? The Law does, of course, teach us to be fair to the foreigner and even uses the same expression.

> When a stranger sojourns with you in your land, you shall not do him wrong. You shall treat the stranger who sojourns with you as the native among you, and you shall love him as yourself, for you were strangers in the land of Egypt: I am the Lord your God.

But, as I have argued before, we are still not to equate the love we show to our own people with this love for the sojourner. Does not Moses teach differences? In Leviticus we are taught that foreign slaves could be bought and kept as slaves forever, but that we can never make a countryman a slave.

Furthermore, look at the basis for treating the sojourner fairly. It is because we were once sojourners in Egypt. We are not blood brothers with them. We are not together the children of the same God. No, indeed. Why, the children of Abraham are the chosen people of God. How could we regard outsiders as our own kind? Are we to regard our oppressors, the Romans, as our neighbors? Are we to regard blasphemers as our neighbors?

Moses warned us of mixing with foreigners. He made clear the danger of succumbing to their pagan ways. Was not our very fall and exile the result of being too close of neighbors? Are not the Samaritans the example of what happens when the blood of different races are mixed? It is better to be a pure-blooded pagan than a mixed-race Samaritan who has desecrated our religion.

I ask many questions. They are all summed up in the question I added: "And who is my neighbor?"

Believe me I was ready with a response if Jesus had asked me how I read the Law. I was ready with whatever answer he might offer. I knew of his love-your-enemy statements. I knew how lenient he was with our oppressors. And I was ready to match argument with argument.

Then Jesus replies with a story. Asking questions and telling parables are not unusual for a Rabbi. I knew the story would make his argument. I listened intently. I would not be caught off guard.

A man was going down from Jerusalem to Jericho, and he fell among robbers, who stripped him and beat him and departed, leaving him half dead. Now by chance a priest was going down that road, and when he saw him he passed by on the other side. So likewise a Levite, when he came to the place and saw him, passed by on the other side.

I knew where Jesus was going with this. Another swipe at religious leaders. The only surprise is that he did not choose a lawyer to be one of the bad guys. These men ought to have treated the injured as a neighbor. The Law is clear about that as well. Take care of the poor, the sick, and the outcast, whoever they might be. I got the picture. But he has the gall to make the most offensive blasphemer the good guy.

But a Samaritan, as he journeyed, came to where he was, and when he saw him, he had compassion.

What is Jesus doing? A Samaritan? A Samaritan? What is he trying to prove?

He went to him and bound up his wounds, pouring on oil and wine.

He is going too far! I am not the only one shocked. His disciples are clearly uneasy. It is one thing to make a cut at us priests and scholars. I can own up to how crabby and proud we can be. Then make a common peasant the compassionate hero. Why a Samaritan?

Then he set him on his own animal and brought him to an inn and took care of him.

Come on, Jesus can't make this guy too good, can he?

And the next day he took out two denarii and gave them to the innkeeper, saying, "Take care of him, and whatever more you spend, I will repay you when I come back."

Seriously? A Samaritan is going to pour out his money for the good of a Jew, for there is no doubt Jesus means us to understand the victim to be. And, really, what innkeeper would have trusted a Samaritan to make good on his promise? The story is totally unrealistic.

As I stewed quietly, Jesus then asked, "Which of these three, do you think, proved to be a neighbor to the man who fell among the robbers?"

The trap opened. "Proved to be a neighbor?" That wasn't the point of my question. Who qualified to be helped? That was the issue. The victim should have been the neighbor in question, not the benefactor. And, if Jesus had made the Samaritan the victim I could have accepted (though not without further debate) that he should be regarded, if not a neighbor, still somehow one who ought to be helped. Help anyone in need. That is the point of the Leviticus law to love the sojourner as myself. And God knows how needy Samaritans are.

Proved to be a neighbor? I was caught off guard. What could I say? "The one who showed him mercy."

"You go, and do likewise." The trap closed.

And then Jesus walked away, his disciples following. I was left alone pondering what had happened.

He had tricked me. The Teacher had outmaneuvered me. He had, well, he had pierced my soul, the very thoughts and intentions of my heart. I wanted debate. He diagnosed my heart. And he gave me a bitter pill to swallow.

Proved to be a neighbor? Could I accept help from such a neighbor? How humiliating that would be! Hhmm…Does mercy work both ways? The giver must be humble enough to give mercy. The receiver must be humble enough to accept it?

This insistence to define who a neighbor might or might not be. Can I really say it comes out of a heart desiring the honor of God? Is the honor of his name at stake or the justification of my pride? To whom will I prove to be a neighbor? In what circumstance will I prove to be a neighbor?

"You go, and do likewise," he said to me.

Perhaps it is time to end the questions and act on the answers.

The Pharisee

And he said, "There was a man who had two sons. And the younger of them said to his father, 'Father, give me the share of property that is coming to me.' And he divided his property between them. Not many days later, the younger son gathered all he had and took a journey into a far country, and there he squandered his property in reckless living."

—Luke 15:11–13

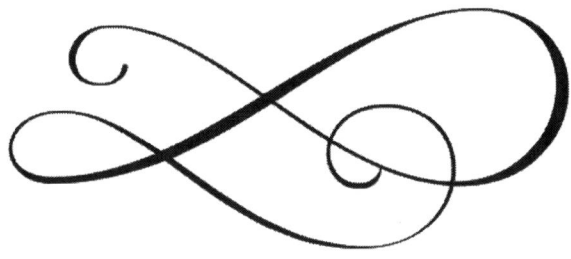

For full story:
Luke 15:11–32

It's all wrong. Every bit of the story is wrong. Oh, I know what Jesus was trying to say. I know the swipe he was taking at me and my brothers. He hates us Pharisees. I know he does. He never has anything good to say about us. Well, if he thought he had scored another point against us, he could not be more mistaken. It is his lack of what is just that is exposed.

Jesus, who puts himself forward as a rabbi, is yet again blatantly showing his disregard for the honor of our God. Why does he dine with tax collectors—traitors to their fellow countrymen—and with, well, we will call them sinners? What they actually do is too shameful to name, though Jesus himself alludes to it with the younger son's "reckless living" with prostitutes.

Again, Jesus gets everything wrong. We are supposed to feel good about the father receiving back the son? Let's see, the younger son had left his father and taken his property. That is bad enough. He squanders the money on prostitutes and whatever else. He only comes to his senses because of his misery. He prepares a speech of false repentance, knowing that he can fool his father. He has done nothing to show that he is deserving of being received back. Nothing, just like these lowlifes that Jesus has a good time with.

The father—and I know who the father is supposed to be, which is nothing short of blasphemy. I am to accept that the Holy One makes a fool of himself running after worthless sinners and then actually celebrating with a party? Is Jesus crazy? Does he have no respect for God's honor? Does he not understand what it means to fear the Lord?

That is all that we Pharisees have ever tried to do—honor the name of the Most High. I know we seem harsh. I know how we are accused of being self-righteous. But at least we are trying to live the righteous life that God demands of all his people. It was because of wanton sin and idolatry that

God sent us into exile, and it no doubt is for the same reason that we live now under the rule of the Romans.

John the Baptist would never have approved of Jesus' behavior. He told it like it was. Repentance is the only way to get right with God. Don't expect any favors; don't expect mercy until you have proven that you are worthy of it.

The elder brother—he should be the hero of the story, not the villain Jesus wants to make of him. This is one time that I am proud of whom Jesus identifies with me. Here is a man who lived by the code of earning his standing before God. What Jesus has him saying is what I desire to say to my God: "many years I have served you, and I never disobeyed your command." I have studied God's law. I have delighted in God's law. I have labored over it to understand it and to obey it. Such a life has been difficult at times, but I have never complained of my lot. I have kept my eyes on the same hope as my fathers—to sit someday at the table with Abraham and Isaac and Jacob in the kingdom of God.

Will God allow prostitutes and adulterers into his kingdom? Will he allow traitors and oppressors? Is God not a God of justice? Shall not the Judge of all the earth do what is just? It is well to speak of mercy. Yes, I knew of his flippant reply when he was earlier called to account for this same behavior. "Go and learn what this means: 'I desire mercy, and not sacrifice.'" If he wants to quote prophets, so can I. "Behold, to obey is better than sacrifice." Those are Samuel's words to Saul as he pronounced the Lord's rejection of him. Saul felt sorry for his disobedience too, but it did him no good.

Mercy cannot ignore justice. God cannot wave his hand to forgive sinners and remain a righteous God. Jesus should know that. There must be repentance. There must be obedience to the law. Neither Hosea nor Samuel were dismissing sacrifices. They were teaching the same lesson—that sacrifice without a repentant and obedient heart does no good. Jesus would do well to quote the prophet Amos:

> I hate, I despise your feasts,
>   and I take no delight in your solemn assemblies.
> Even though you offer me your burnt offerings and grain

> offerings,
> I will not accept them;
> and the peace offerings of your fattened animals,
> I will not look upon them.
> Take away from me the noise of your songs;
> to the melody of your harps I will not listen.
> But let justice roll down like waters,
> and righteousness like an ever-flowing stream.

Where is justice in this story of his? The sinner is treated as a prince; the father acts like a fool; and the good son is held up as the villain.

Lost? The son was not lost. He had run away. He had rebelled. Only his misery made him return. And he gets a royal welcome. Oh, I gladly identify with the elder son. I have not rebelled. I have remained obedient. I have kept my nose to the grind. No parties for me, which this Jesus seems to enjoy. Is not what they say about him true—that he is a glutton and a drunkard? If I were the elder brother I would not have accepted a party if my father had offered me one, not after the disgrace of the younger brother's party.

Why this insistence to be friends with sinners before they make changes in their lives? He told two parables before this one and each time concludes that heaven rejoices over a sinner who repents. I've got no problem with that lesson. But there is no real repentance in this story, and, even if the son had repented, the father clearly welcomed him before the son had time to speak. I remember how Jesus described it: "But while he was still a long way off, his father saw him and felt compassion, and ran and embraced him and kissed him."

It is this unseemly eagerness of a holy God to welcome sinners that I cannot condone. I am as welcoming as anyone of a sinner who has repented, made his sacrifice, and over time has demonstrated a changed life. The father should have had his son do what he supposedly planned to do—work as a servant. The son should have earned his acceptance, and he should have paid back the money he had taken. Then the father could have afforded to show mercy.

Now that I think about it, there is a sacrifice in the story. No doubt Jesus is oblivious to it. The fatted calf was sacrificed. It was killed for the benefit of the worthless son. A real sacrifice was needed. Doesn't Jesus understand what sacrifices are about? Someone, something must pay the price for forgiveness. Mercy does not come without a cost. Without the shedding of blood there is no forgiveness of sins.

Surely he must understand this principle. That is what the daily sacrifices are for. That is why the people continually bring animals to the temple for sacrifice. That is the whole point of the Day of Atonement. That is the lesson of the Passover lamb. God cannot simply forgive a sinner because the sinner wants to be forgiven. A sacrifice must be made. God's just wrath must be satisfied if he is to remain a just God. Why can't Jesus get this into his head?

He likes to call God his Father. He would do well to behave as a son who does his father's will.

The Rich, Young Ruler

And as he was setting out on his journey, a man ran up and knelt before him and asked him, "Good Teacher, what must I do to inherit eternal life?"

—Mark 10:17

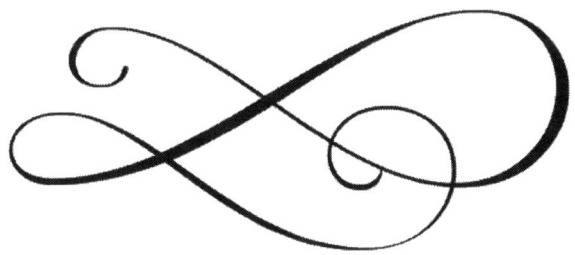

For full story:
Mark 10:17–27

J ob was rich; so were our fathers Abraham, Isaac, and Jacob. Riches were blessings that the Lord bestowed upon them. Why then would Jesus compel me to give up mine? If I had obtained my wealth through oppression of the poor and through theft or breaking any of the commandments, I could understand such a demand. But what had I done wrong? Why must I be called upon to give up what everyone else recognizes as God's blessing on a life well lived?

I came to this teacher in good faith. I was not as some who had been trying to trick him, pretending to want to learn when they really wanted to discredit him. When I addressed him as Good Teacher, I meant what I said. I was addressing him with due respect. Even that he turned against me. "Why do you call me good? No one is good but God alone." Well, yes, that is true but he was taking my respectful address out of context.

Even so, my question also was sincere: What good deed must I do to inherit eternal life? This has been the one concern that has motivated all I have done in life. I grew up not merely hearing the law taught, but with the urgent desire to observe the law and all for the purpose of attaining my heavenly inheritance promised in the law.

I was not like many of my friends who paid lip-service to the law, assuming that they would enter into the kingdom of heaven merely because they were born into the covenant and circumcised. They would laugh at my efforts to be good. Some were mean-spirited about it and accused me of being self-righteous. But I loved the law. No one accused King David of being self-righteous. I wanted to be like him—a ruler who loved the law and committed to ruling justly. And so I have done what I could in my small sphere of rule to see that justice and fair dealing is played out.

The Rich, Young Ruler

But to get back to my question, although I seem to have all the bases covered, I have nevertheless not felt that I could rest completely on the matter. There are, after all, so many laws. What if I was missing something? I did not think I had but one never knows. I have actually asked this same question of many religious teachers, and everyone has assured me that I am on the right track. But it never hurts to ask one more teacher.

And this teacher was different. I had been told of his teaching with authority—teaching backed up with miraculous healings. No one did the things he did; no one taught like he did; all the more, then, it seemed good to bring my question to him.

When I asked my question, he gave the response of the other teachers. Keep the commandments. So far so good. I asked which ones, and he gave the standard summary—do not murder, do not commit adultery, do not steal, do not lie, do not defraud, honor my parents. I had heard these before and was feeling pretty good because I had been observing every one of these laws. So when I replied that I had been keeping them, I was expecting the same response as from the other teachers—an assurance that I was already doing what needed to be done. Indeed, not to be boastful, but every similar conversation ended with the teacher commending me for my strict observance of the law, and usually they would note that my riches signified God's favor on me.

The teacher did not respond immediately. He looked at me; he looked at me as though trying to see inside of me. I felt awkward, and yet, by his look I could tell that he really cared about me. He was taking me seriously; he was taking the whole matter of attaining heaven seriously. What at first had seemed almost academic was a matter of greatest importance.

"You lack one thing."

"Yes?" What is this one thing I lacked? I had always sensed there was something I was missing. What is it?

"Go, sell all that you have and give to the poor, and you will have treasure in heaven; and come, follow me."

I was stunned. Give to the poor? I had done that my whole life. I tithed more than the ten percent. I always gave alms to beggars. I never refused anyone. No one was more conscientious than I in almsgiving. But I was willing to do more. I had a field or two I could have sold if needed. There were some other possessions I could have given up.

But sell *all* that I had? *All* that I possessed? Did he not know who I was and what I possessed? Don't misunderstand me, I am a humble man, but also a realistic man. It is one thing for poor fishermen to give up their meager possessions, but would they have done the same if wealthy? If they had come from a prosperous and distinguished family such as I, would they have so glibly walked away from it?

And I was not merely being asked to walk away from my possessions. I was to sell them, dispose of them so that I had nothing to go back to. Even now those fisherman could have gone back to their jobs. This wealth had been in my family; was I to toss away what my father had worked hard to produce? How could I honor my parents by giving away my inheritance?

I was to sell my possessions. That is not simple to do. I have much. I can't just hold an estate sale and get rid of it all. It would take weeks, maybe months to dispose of it properly. Sell my possessions? The very word is odious. Sell my possessions as though they were mere merchandise and not precious heirlooms?

It wasn't a question of security. I do not really trust in my riches, certainly not more than I trust the Lord. I know that God will provide. But is this not how he is providing for me? I do not put myself above common men, even poor men, but on what basis am I to toss away what my God has blessed me with? And would he not have blessed me unless I was already obeying his will?

I am a reasonable man. If this Jesus had provided good reason; if he had quoted Scripture, I would have considered his suggestion. But all he has to say is, "Come, follow me."

Okay, I would have followed him. I can walk long distances. I can live simply. I could take time off. In fact, if he had been reasonable, I could have followed and provided for him and his disciples. Look, I understand the simple lifestyle that a religious teacher like him would follow, and I could adapt to it. But why give up *all* my possessions? Why not let my steward keep watch over my possessions while I am following Jesus? Is that not reasonable? I could see that we give to every street beggar that we pass. If Jesus is so hung up on the poor, then why not let me use my wealth in a practical manner to support his ministry and help his precious poor. Why this foolish insistence on selling my possessions? I lose my possessions and the money is spent up immediately as it always is when wasted on the poor. I don't mean wasted, but we all know that there will be more mouths to feed than we can help and once the money is used up, the poor remain poor and hungry. I just don't get it.

I walked away, and the teacher didn't even try to call me back. We probably could have come to some agreement, some reasonable compromise. Just who did he think he was, anyhow? He is a teacher! It's not like he is the Messiah. I respect him for who he is; could he not pay me some respect?

I had not walked out of hearing range when I heard his remark about a camel passing through the eye of a needle being easier than a rich man entering the kingdom of God. Even his disciples were stunned at the remark, as they should have been. "Who then can be saved?" they asked. That is what I had wanted to know. And I still don't know. Jesus told them, "With man this is impossible, but not with God; all things are possible with God."

I walked on, hearing no more.

Zacchaeus

He entered Jericho and was passing through. And behold, there was a man named Zacchaeus. He was a chief tax collector and was rich. And he was seeking to see who Jesus was...

—Luke 19:1–3

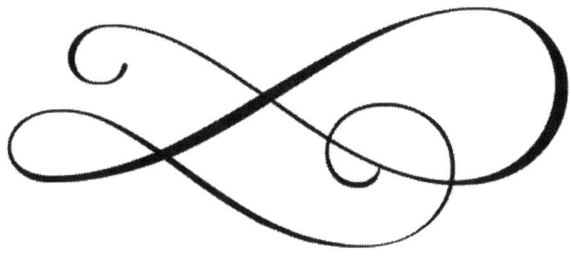

For full story:
Luke 19:1–10

"Son of Abraham"—that's what he called me—Son of Abraham! I have been given other epithets—Traitor, Thief, Son of the Devil. I dare say they were appropriate. I was all those things, more so than the scorners knew. Most of them could see me only from their limited perspective.

The poor, who were the majority, simply resented me for taking their money. They merely saw me as greedy. The religious leaders, especially the Pharisees, saw a sinner who defiled himself by association with the Gentiles and morally loose companions. They all regarded me as a traitor, although I could tell that the Sadducees understood the complexity of my service for the Romans. All of them were right. I certainly was greedy. Why else go into the tax collecting business? And even I at the time knew how morally loose I was. I had a ball engaging in those loose morals.

But my detractors could not penetrate deeper into my heart. They might have seen cynicism, but they did not see the bitter resentment that brewed in me. Greedy? Yes, but for more than money. I was greedy for respect. That might make you laugh, seeing how little respect I appeared to have. But rest assured, I had a respect that instilled fear in everyone, from the lowest peasant to the highest man of means. That is what my connection with the Romans gave me. However much I might be hated, I was protected. And I felt powerful.

I was somebody! I actually convinced myself enough to feel that way… for a time. It couldn't last—the feeling, that is. How powerful can you feel when you must always watch your back? How satisfying can such respect be when you know that you are the butt of private jokes and the object of hate? And my morally loose friends? They are loose friends, laughing at my jokes and attending my parties as long as I keep my position. As great a fool as

I was, even I knew that the Romans protected me only as long as I turned in the quotas that they kept raising.

And so all the more I schemed, intimidated, deceived, and cheated. Being a real sinner takes more than half-way measures. I must heap sin upon sin to protect myself and to hold on to what I have.

I had heard about Jesus of Nazareth. He was a miracle worker. News came in regularly about the latest. He healed the lame; he drove out demons; he cleansed lepers; he gave sight to the blind. There was even a claim that he had brought back to life some who had died. That, I knew, was over the top, but still…many of his miracles must have been real. Maybe someday he would come here to Jericho. He lived in Galilee, and this is the town that pilgrims passed through to Jerusalem when they went around Samaria.

Yes, it would be intriguing to see the miracle worker, but other news came in that really caught my interest. Someone reported that this Jesus had actually touched lepers to cleanse them. Touch lepers? He would dare touch such outcasts? He was evidently, too, getting on the wrong side of the religious leaders, who were warning the people not to listen to him. If he had their enmity, he must be someone worth knowing.

And then one night at my house party, his name came up. It was true that the religious establishment had turned against him, especially because he was associating with sinners. Really? This so-called prophet of God was associating with sinners like us? That couldn't be true. But one of the tax collectors that subcontracted with me affirmed it. Jesus had actually attended the party of one of the tax collectors he knew up in Galilee.

That was incredible to believe. No self-respecting rabbi would pass me by on the same side of the road, much less condescend to speak to me. Dining in a tax collector's home was as believable as Jesus raising someone from the dead.

"But it is true!" my associate exclaimed. "The Teacher has even chosen a tax collector to be his disciple!"

We all laughed at such a preposterous statement. But he insisted it was true. He even knew the man's name—Levi, who served in the Capernaum district. A couple of others then spoke up. They had known Levi and heard that he had left the business but didn't know why.

Could this be true? Could this man of God be a friend of sinners? Who has ever heard of such a thing? He certainly was a man worth meeting.

The day finally came that Jesus of Nazareth was passing through Jericho. Passover was near and the pilgrims from Galilee were traveling through the town every day. It was a noisy, crazy time when the town was mobbed by thousands of visitors. I was specially kept busy overseeing my subcontractors who were manning their toll booths. My most profitable time of the year!

I was in my home going over the collection records when an associate rushed in. "The Prophet! He is coming!"

I ran out with him, though we were quickly separated in the crowds. It would have been crowded enough with the parade of pilgrims, but now that word had gotten out about Jesus, everyone was out trying to catch a glimpse of him. And I could see nothing.

Did I mention that I am not exactly tall? There were some epithets that referred to my short stature, as well. I may have been short but I was also shrewd, and I knew what to do. I knew the sycamore tree under which Jesus had to pass. I made my way through the crowd to the tree, climbed up, and perched with the best view in town.

I looked ahead. Yes, that must be him where the people were pressing in. Those must be his disciples who are trying to clear a path. I wondered if Levi was one of them. They are getting nearer along the route I expected. I see him clearly now. He is almost underneath me. He's looking at me.

"Zacchaeus, hurry and come down, for I must stay at your house today."

I suppose I should have been startled that he knew my name, but it was his invitation...well, actually he was inviting himself to my house. My house! He didn't exactly ask; it was more of an urgent statement: "I must stay at your house today." It was as if he was compelled to act immediately. "Hurry and come down."

Be sure I did hurry! I scrambled down the tree as quickly as I could. Me! Jesus chose me among all the throng that were trying to see him and touch him. Me! I was more surprised than the townspeople who were grumbling in disdain. "He has gone in to be the guest of a man who is a sinner." That's right! Jesus declared that he would be my guest, the most despised sinner in the town.

It was true—all of those reports that this was one man of God who openly befriended defamed sinners. We had no trouble walking to my house. The people pulled away from us since I was leading the way. No one wanted to be near me!

What happened then in my house? We shared a meal. He told some of his stories. But it was not so much what he said as it was the way he treated me—as though I were true to my heritage—that of belonging to God's covenant people. Indeed, you might have mistaken me for one of his disciples.

The commitment I made with my tithes and of making amends for what I had defrauded the people…well, what of it? Yes, it turned out to be a lot of money—enough even to nearly wipe out my possessions. But, then again, what of it? My Lord came into my house and received me as a true son of Abraham—me, whom even I had given up as a son of the devil, too far gone, too great a sinner. Through Jesus of Nazareth God had answered the private prayer of my heart—Have mercy on me, a sinner.

Nathaniel at Jesus' Triumphant Entry

They brought the donkey and the colt and put on them their cloaks, and he sat on them. Most of the crowd spread their cloaks on the road, and others cut branches from the trees and spread them on the road. And the crowds that went before him and that followed him were shouting, "Hosanna to the Son of David! Blessed is he who comes in the name of the Lord! Hosanna in the highest!"

—Matthew 21:7–9

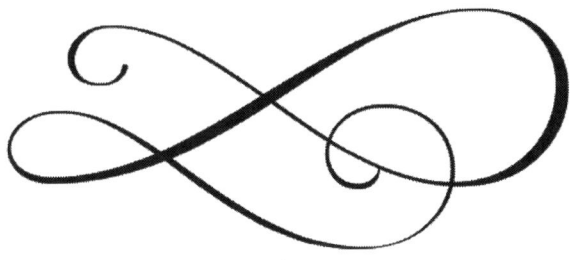

For full story:
Matthew 21:1–17

This is the greatest day of my life! What a glorious day! We have entered Jerusalem, the city of David, and our Lord, the Son of David, has received the acclaim that we have been waiting for.

Nearly three years have gone by since we began to follow Jesus of Nazareth. I remember well the day, relaxing under a fig tree, that Philip came to me excited. "We have found him of whom Moses in the Law and also the prophets wrote, Jesus of Nazareth, the son of Joseph."

I groaned. Both Philip and I were eager for the Messiah to come. We have studied the Scriptures and listened attentively to the teachings of rabbis. In our day there has been a growing anticipation of his coming. Many believe that he will come in our generation. There have been two or three names rumored to be the Messiah. Philip and I have wondered about the prophet known as John the Baptist.

But a Jesus of Nazareth? Seriously, that hick town? What Scripture speaks of any leader coming out of Nazareth, much less the Messiah. Some rabbis teach that the Messiah would be born in Bethlehem, the town of David, but I agreed with others that he would come suddenly out of nowhere. Nazareth? He has a father named Joseph? Who is Joseph?

I scoffed: ""Can anything good come out of Nazareth?"

Philip would not be put off, and so I reluctantly followed him. We turned a corner. Philip pointed him out to me. He seemed like an ordinary man. As we drew near he said, "Behold, an Israelite indeed, in whom there is no deceit!" I must admit, I was flattered.

"How do you know me?" I expected him to say something about my looks or that Philip had told him about me.

"Before Philip called you, when you were under the fig tree, I saw you."

I stared at him. He looked straight back. It was clear that in him there was no deceit. He was telling the truth. He undid me. "Rabbi, you are the Son of God! You are the King of Israel!"

Looking back, I did get carried away. But as I said, I was eager and ready to believe the Messiah would come. And he did appear as out of nowhere. No trumpets, no angels, no army about him. Jesus of Nazareth, son of Joseph, laughed—a head back, joyous laugh.

"Because I said to you, 'I saw you under the fig tree,' do you believe? You will see greater things than these."

The laughter ended. He looked intensely at me. "Truly, truly, I say to you, you will see heaven opened, and the angels of God ascending and descending on the Son of Man."

I could not help but look up. We both grinned. From that day I followed Jesus looking for the day when heaven would open. It could not be long. Three years later I still wait.

I have to admit that I have wondered at times if we were mistaken. Jesus did perform miracles—wondrous miracles, but what were they leading to? He should have had an army by now. The people have been ready to crown him king. But each time that the moment has seemed ripe for his revealing, he moves on.

And then this talk of his about being killed in Jerusalem. Killed? The Messiah? I expect battles and even followers dying on his behalf, but the Messiah be killed in the city of David? Where is that to be found in the Scriptures?

But now, finally, such fears can be put to rest. What a glorious day! Jesus had sent me and Philip early this morning to a nearby village to procure a colt. We obeyed eagerly, for we knew the significance of what he was doing. We know the prophecy of Zechariah.

> Rejoice greatly, O daughter of Zion!
>   Shout aloud, O daughter of Jerusalem!
> Behold, your king is coming to you;
>   righteous and having salvation is he,
> humble and mounted on a donkey,
>   on a colt, the foal of a donkey.

All went exactly as he told us. The colt, the permission of the owner—everything fell into place. More important than the colt being ready was that our Master finally was accepting his calling. We knew that he knew the prophecy and that he intended to enter Jerusalem as king.

And he has! In our excitement we—his followers—spread our garments on the animal and even on the path that the colt tread. Others cut branches and placed them on the road. We sang Psalm 118, and then some began to shout out, "Hosanna to the Son of David! Blessed is he who comes in the name of the Lord! Hosanna in the highest!"

The crowds that were entering with us joined in the shouts and spreading branches when they realized who was sitting on the colt. "There is the prophet who raised Lazarus from the dead!" "There is the Messiah!"

We enter through the gates. Someone calls out, "This is the prophet Jesus from Nazareth of Galilee!" Philip and I laughed heartily. Yes, Jesus of Nazareth! And make no mistake, this Jesus the son of Joseph is the Son of David!

Jesus was wonderful. He soon hopped off the colt and then marched straight to the temple. All the while is the continual singing of Psalm 118. It had begun as we neared the gates and echoed in the city along the path to the temple.

> Blessed is he who comes in the name of the Lord!
> We bless you from the house of the Lord.
> The Lord is God,
> and he has made his light to shine upon us.
> Bind the festal sacrifice with cords,
> up to the horns of the altar!

Is that what he was going to do—offer his sacrifice of thanksgiving? Or was he marching to his coronation? Will heaven open? I looked up to the sky.

We arrived. Jesus marched up the steps and into the section where the animals for sacrifice were sold. I thought he was going to purchase his sacrifice. But no, he began to turn over the tables of the moneychangers! He grabbed a whip of cords and struck out at the animal sellers! He knocked over cages and stools. He was like a madman! No, not like a madman; like the king that he was driving out the unrighteous who defiled the temple. "It is written, 'My house shall be a house of prayer'; but you have made it a den of robbers!"

This is the action of the Messiah, the Anointed of God come to purify his people and to protect the honor of God's name. I looked up. Will heaven open? He has been confronted by the priests. They challenge his authority. Will he now call down his angels? I looked up.

"Destroy this temple and in three days I will raise it up." Philip and I looked at each other in befuddlement.

Jesus walked away. He was quickly surrounded by those who are sick and by children. They could be in the Court of the Gentiles. And as always, he healed them all—the blind, the lame, all who came to him. And as he did, the children shouted the words they had heard: "Hosanna to the Son of David!"

Again, Jesus was confronted. "Make these children stop." I love his reply: "Have you never read,

'Out of the mouth of infants and nursing babies
you have prepared praise'?"

If they were silent, the very stones would cry out!"

Yes, yes, yes! This is no solemn Jesus. This is no "I must suffer" Jesus. This is the triumphant Messiah ready to ascend his throne as rightful king. I looked up. Will heaven open?

No, not yet. But it must be soon. We have returned to Bethany to the home of Lazarus and his sisters. They have prepared a dinner for us. I like to think of it as Jesus' coronation dinner. It cannot be long before he takes his throne. Heaven must open then. Angels must descend and overthrow all enemies and all the unrighteous. It will be then that my confession will be the confession of everyone, that Jesus of Nazareth is the Son of God, the King of Israel!"

I am looking up.

Mary, the Sister of Martha

Six days before the Passover, Jesus therefore came to Bethany, where Lazarus was, whom Jesus had raised from the dead. So they gave a dinner for him there. Martha served, and Lazarus was one of those reclining with him at table. Mary therefore took a pound of expensive ointment made from pure nard, and anointed the feet of Jesus and wiped his feet with her hair.

—John 12:1–3

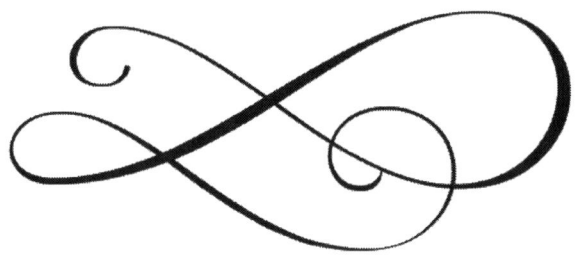

For full story:
John 12:1–8

I knew what I was doing. I was, indeed, anointing his body for burial. I may be young. I may be a woman. But I have listened to Jesus teach. I have observed him as he taught. I understand what lies before him.

From that first time he visited our house I perceived that he was more than a rabbi. No one ever taught with the authority as he, but it was not just the authority that demanded my attention. There was his depth of insight into the kingdom of God unlike any other teacher. And then, something more, something…what was it? The tone of his voice? The expressions on his face? He spoke not as a rabbi who has studied the Scriptures about the kingdom but as a son of the king teaching what his country back home is like.

I had intended to help my sister, Martha, with the preparations. I understood my role. The men gathered to listen to Jesus teach while we women and servants prepared the meal just outside the circle. But when he began to speak, "The kingdom of God is…," I could not help but listen. I do not know how I ended up at his feet. I do not recall anyone or anything else other than his teaching and his voice and his face.

The kingdom of God is like a mustard seed…like a sower sowing seeds…like a treasure in the field…like a fine pearl. Such imagery I had never heard. He spoke of belonging to the kingdom. There were the righteous, yes, but also those who mourned, those who are humble like children, those who are children, those who are poor, those (I was startled) who are tax collectors and prostitutes.

The kingdom of God is at hand. I think I gasped at those words. The kingdom of God was at hand because he was here! What else could he mean except that he was the Messiah, the Anointed One!

My sister—what is she doing there beside Jesus?

"Lord, do you not care that my sister has left me to serve alone? Tell her then to help me."

Oh my! She's right! I had forgotten my place and duty. I looked around. The men were staring at me. I started to get up when Jesus replied,

"Martha, Martha, you are anxious and troubled about many things, but one thing is necessary. Mary has chosen the good portion, which will not be taken away from her."

I was moved but embarrassed. I did not want to upset my sister, and I could see that she herself was embarrassed by Jesus' remark. She hurried away. I quietly rose, bowed to Jesus, and then joined Martha. She was clearly upset. We did not speak as I helped with preparations. The next day, however, I could see a change in her. When Jesus began to teach, she actually sat with me and listened. We have had many conversations since.

We saw Jesus on occasion afterwards. He and our brother, Lazarus, became good friends. We heard more teaching. We did not see but we did hear about his miracles. Many healings and driving out demons. The disciples shared with us about his calming the storm and walking on water. He even multiplied food for thousands. It was clear to all of us that Jesus was the Messiah and that he would soon establish the kingdom of God. The kingdom! We were near the great Day of Judgment when the dead would rise. We must be. What else could Jesus' coming mean?

And yet, as excited as Jesus' disciples would be, I never saw the same look of expectation in him. He spoke of the kingdom to come, yet the stories were not about power and glory but how we should live in such a kingdom. The kingdom would grow quietly, even humbly. Yes, at times he spoke of the Son of Man coming with the angels, but then, what did that mean except that Jesus would go away for a time? Where would he go?

One time I heard him tell his disciples that the Son of Man must suffer and be killed and yet on the third day be raised. No one questioned him. They were flustered by the remark and did not want to pursue it. But it must be important. Why else say it? All the more carefully I listened and observed him.

Then came the day that Lazarus became ill. His fever rose rapidly. We knew that without a miracle he would die. We sent for Jesus and waited. The next day our brother died. How could this happen? How could God let it happen? Where was Jesus? We buried him. It would be four days later when Jesus arrived and performed his greatest miracle of raising our brother from the dead. With my very own eyes I saw him come out of the tomb. Who but the Messiah, the Son of God, could possess such power? Martha later told me what he had said to her.

"I am the resurrection and the life. Whoever believes in me, though he die, yet shall he live, and everyone who lives and believes in me shall never die."

Now, all of Jesus' followers are excited. He has entered Jerusalem with the welcome of a triumphant king. The kingdom is at hand, so it seems. Why then has his excitement not risen, as well? We live not far from the city, and he has returned to our house. We planned a dinner of thanks for his good deed for Lazarus.

I could see that he is troubled, that he increasingly seems weighed down with a grief. I have remembered that remark of how he would suffer and be killed. I have never stopped contemplating it and searching the Scriptures for understanding. I have found the answer in the prophet Isaiah.

> Surely he has borne our griefs
>   and carried our sorrows;
> yet we esteemed him stricken,
>   smitten by God, and afflicted.
> But he was pierced for our transgressions;
>   he was crushed for our iniquities;
> upon him was the chastisement that brought us peace,
>   and with his wounds we are healed.

The Anointed One is the Suffering Servant, and his time is at hand. No one else seems to understand, and I can see the burden of my Lord bearing his grief alone.

We have had a jar of nard, a sweet-fragrant perfume that has been saved in our family. We had thought that it might be used someday for a wedding, though none of us three have had such cause to use it. I took it upon myself to use it for our Lord. This can be my fault—to act impulsively—and yet, nothing seemed more appropriate, even planned, than this act.

As I said, I knew what I was doing. I know that he is to die, even if no one else can or refuses to acknowledge it. I have anointed the Anointed One. As Jesus has said correctly, I have prepared his body for burial. He must know that someone—someone who loves him—understands his grief, that he is not alone in bearing it.

He must know that someone honors him for the humiliation that he will soon endure. He must know that someone thanks him for his sacrifice. I do not trust Judas. I have observed him, as well. His heart is not right.

The Passover is near. Yes, I see now more clearly how the time is at hand. The Anointed One is the Passover Lamb. It is for this purpose that my Lord has come into this world, to taste the death that should be ours, to be pierced for our transgressions.

I look back to that first night, sitting at his feet, enrapt with the thrill that the Teacher was the Messiah. I had forgotten my place, oblivious even to my surroundings. Now, now that I understand what being the Messiah entails, I am taken into far deeper reflection. I feel grief. I feel wonder. I see that my Lord must suffer and be killed. I see that what he did for my brother was but a sign of a greater rising from the dead. He shall rise. He shall return again. That is what he has taught.

Yes, my anointing is preparation for his burial. It is also preparation for his ascension to the throne. Jesus is the Messiah who some day will sit upon the throne of the kingdom of God. My Teacher has taught me well.

PART THREE

CHRIST DIED

The Angel in the Garden

And he came out and went, as was his custom, to the Mount of Olives, and the disciples followed him. And when he came to the place, he said to them, "Pray that you may not enter into temptation." And he withdrew from them about a stone's throw, and knelt down and prayed, saying, "Father, if you are willing, remove this cup from me. Nevertheless, not my will, but yours, be done." And there appeared to him an angel from heaven, strengthening him.

—Luke 22:39–43

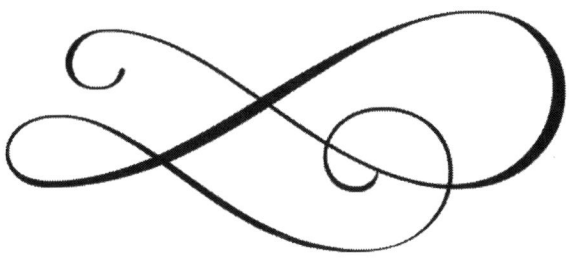

For full story:
Matthew 26:36–56; Luke 22:39–44

I was there for him. I did not fall asleep and leave him alone in his agony. I was not like his disciples who swore devotion, to even die with him. They could not even keep awake with the Master in the time of his greatest need for companionship. And when the moment was at hand to stand with their Lord when his enemies came upon him, they fled away, leaving their vows to die with him on the ground.

I was there for him even as his so-called three closest disciples slept. He had warned them to beware of their own temptation. He had prepared them for the event of that very evening. And yet they slept. They could not keep prayer with their Lord for one hour.

Why had my Lord chosen these feeble men of flesh to be his followers? Why Peter, the most foolish of them all with his bragging of bravery and devotion? All of us angels could see that he was most likely to fail. His silly talk of dying with his Master was but obvious bravado. Hadn't Jesus seen this already? I suppose he had, otherwise he would not have had to pray for Peter when Satan vied for a turn with him.

I was there for Jesus, just as all of us angels were. His words were not bravado when he told the disciples that he could appeal to his Father to send twelve legions of angels. Ha! We had to be held back! We are watching the whole scene unfold. The silly disciples sleeping while our Master prayed. I at least was allowed to come down and do what I could do to strengthen him in his distress. Even so, his sweat became like great drops of blood dripping to the ground.

Three times Jesus had to wake his disciples. Three times! Couldn't they see his distress? Couldn't at least one of them keep their eyes open? All the while, we see the band of soldiers proceeding up the hill led by the traitor, another disciple. What is it with these men? Why are they so fickle? One betrays, another denies, and they all run away? Do their vows mean nothing?

I was there, and I would have remained there for my Master. These are not words of bravado. I certainly did not fear human soldiers. But I would have remained if Satan had sent his legions of fallen angels. Yes, even angels have fallen but not since the great rebellion. Satan could not infect all of us as he has infected all humans.

Why had the Son of God come to this moment? He is God, equal with God the Father and God the Spirit. He did not have to leave his place in glory. What was at stake? God's glory was not diminished by the fall. The Blessed Trinity did not need paltry man for anything. They had one another in eternal perfect fellowship. And they still have us—the angels who have remained true. We come before the very throne of God and worship him in holiness and righteousness and unpolluted love and devotion.

Why did the Son take on mortal flesh? Why leave his home in glory? For whom? For what? These fickle, feeble humans? The best desert him. They had been with Jesus three years listening to him, watching him, experiencing life with him—had they learned nothing?

Why was I only allowed to do so little? I groaned with him. I heard his prayer. "My Father, if it be possible, let this cup pass from me; nevertheless, not as I will, but as you will." Why could the cup not be passed? He did not want to drink it. Why must the Son of God drink the bitter cup? I could have taken it for him. No, no…I got caught in the moment like that silly Peter did. The cup given to the Son—only he was capable of drinking such a bitter draft.

And the Son was committed to the will of the Father. So why did the Father not take it away? How could he have his Son drink the cup of death? Doesn't he see his Son's anguish? Doesn't he love his Son? How could the Father listen to his Son, watch the silly soldiers walk up the hill, and do nothing?

He sent me? Well, yes, but not to defend the Son, merely to strengthen him so that he would drink the cup. I wanted to do more. I wanted to slay those soldiers. I wanted to wake up the disciples with a wakeup call that they would not forget. I wanted to bring my Master back home where he belonged.

But that was not the Father's will, and the Son listened only to the Father. I would have thought that he listened begrudgingly if were not for his earlier prayer that same night before crossing over to Gethsemane. He spoke of these weak followers as though they were gifts from the Father. He prayed for their protection; he prayed for their unity; he prayed for them to know the Father's love just as he knew his Father's love; he prayed for them to be with him in glory.

No, I have to admit that God the Son was kneeling in the garden, sweating blood because he desired with his Father the salvation of these foolish disciples and all others like them who believe in him with their weak faith. The cup could have passed if either the Son or the Father had faltered in willing the sleeping men's salvation. The cup could have passed if either had had enough of denial and treason and abandonment. We legions of angels could have executed Judgment Day then and there if the Father had but said it was time.

But it was not time. It was not the hour of judgment but of salvation. The Son would do more than sweat blood; he would shed his blood. He would lift the cup with his own hands and drink it fully to the last dregs. He would do so, not because I strengthened him. Who am I to strengthen the Son of God, even in his flesh? No, he would do so because he willed to do the Father's will which already was his own. He would drink bitterness because of the joy that was set before him and for which he had prayed—that he would be glorified and that all whom his Father has given him will be with him forever in glory.

Hhmm...and so they will be with me. These sleeping disciples will enter the land where there is no sleep. They will join me in the throne room, in the heavenly sanctuary and sing with me the glorious anthems to the Father and the Son, who is something new—the Lamb. Together we will sing the new song:

> Worthy is the Lamb who was slain,
> to receive power and wealth and wisdom and might
> and honor and glory and blessing!

Nathaniel in the Garden

Now as they were eating, Jesus took bread, and after blessing it broke it and gave it to the disciples, and said, "Take, eat; this is my body." And he took a cup, and when he had given thanks he gave it to them, saying, "Drink of it, all of you, for this is my blood of the covenant, which is poured out for many for the forgiveness of sins. I tell you I will not drink again of this fruit of the vine until that day when I drink it new with you in my Father's kingdom." And when they had sung a hymn, they went out to the Mount of Olives. Then Jesus said to them, "You will all fall away because of me this night."

—Matthew 26:27–31

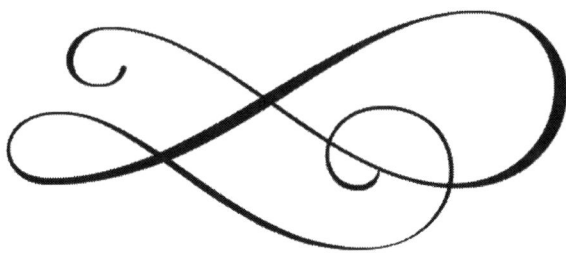

For full story:
Matthew 26:17–46

I don't understand what's going on. Nothing has made sense this evening. I am tired, so very tired.

Nothing has gone right ever since we entered Jerusalem. Each day I think is the day that Jesus will reveal himself and the angels will come down. Each day I wait for the display of his power. All we have done is to go to the temple for Jesus to teach. That's it, nothing more, except for the confrontations with the religious leaders. Their hostility toward him increases, especially as he has embarrassed them in every argument.

I thought that perhaps this evening would be the event of his revelation. It was clear that he looked with anticipation to the dinner, that he had prepared for it as he had the entry into the city. It would make sense. Just as the Passover begins the Deliverer of Israel rises up. Jesus was just biding his time. Or maybe tonight would be the preparation night. Jesus would reveal his plan to us, and we would prepare for his coronation. He certainly was planning something. We could see in his face a growing intensity as for a momentous event about to take place.

We gathered in that upper room. From the beginning everything Jesus did seemed out of place. He washed our feet, as if he were nothing more than our servant. It was embarrassing. This is not the way for a king to behave. It is fine and well to talk about serving one another, but Jesus is our King; he is the King of Israel. Isn't he?

And then there was the meal itself. He takes the bread, breaks it, and then parcels it out to us with the comment, "Take eat, this is my body given for you." His body? What does that mean? It sounds like the odd words he had spoken to us long ago: "The bread that I give for the life of the world is my flesh." We never have understood what he was talking about then. The bread his body? He should have been talking battle strategy. He should have been preparing us for the angels coming down.

And then he takes a cup of wine. "Drink. This is the blood of the new covenant, which is poured out for you and for many for the forgiveness of sins." There they were again, his earlier words: "Whoever feeds on my flesh and drinks my blood has eternal life." What did all this mean? I can understand the new covenant. We were looking for it through the Messiah, when the law of God would be written on our hearts. But I don't understand about the blood. Yes, there would be many sacrifices of animals lifted up in the new kingdom, but Jesus was referring to his own. Did he mean that his blood would be shed as he fought against our enemies? Is that it? But he speaks of us drinking his blood. And how does his shed blood bring about forgiveness of sins? This is not battle talk. I want to hear about the legion of angels that should be coming down.

It was already a somber room when he delivered the crushing news. He was to be betrayed by one of us. Betrayed? What is Jesus talking about? Who could do such a thing? We looked suspiciously at one another. No doubt each of us wanted to say, "Is it he?" but we knew that would not go over well with the Teacher who had just demonstrated being a servant. And so, one by one, "Is it I?"

He merely looked at us with gloomy eyes. "You will all fall away, for it is written, 'I will strike the shepherd, and the sheep will be scattered.'" He said something else, but I cannot remember.

This was too much for Peter. "Even though they all fall away, I will not!" We rolled our eyes ready for Jesus' rebuke. This would not be the first time, but what he said took us all back.

"Peter, I tell you this very night you will deny me three times."

Peter was beside himself. "If I must die with you, I will not deny you." We were all aroused. We all protested our courage. And we mean it. I do. I am ready to die with my Lord.

I am so tired. What is going on with Jesus? What does he mean to do? So much he has said to us tonight even as we have left the house and walked up the hill. He speaks as if he is going away, as if he is leaving us. Is this all of his plan? Perhaps he must go away to recruit his army. But, then, why wouldn't he take us? Maybe he has a hideout that he is going to as he prepares for his dramatic revealing. Then why not tell us?

No, something is wrong, very wrong. The shepherd will be struck down and the sheep will be scattered. Those warnings come back. "The Son of Man must suffer and be killed." Teacher has not been anticipating his coronation. He has been anticipating his death. And soon! Is it tonight?

I am so tired. Think, think. It is almost as if Jesus has been planning his own defeat. "I must go to Jerusalem and suffer and be killed." He talked about the kingdom, even tonight. He said that he would not taste the fruit of the vine until he tasted it new in the kingdom of God. And yet, didn't he make it clear that he would taste death? His blood is to be poured out.

It is all so confusing. A new kingdom that comes through death. A body to be eaten; blood to be drunk. A king who is a servant. A leader whose followers desert him. A conqueror marching to his death. This is not what I envisioned long ago when I acclaimed him Son of God, King of Israel. This is not what any of us signed up for. We signed up to sit on thrones next to our king over the twelve tribes of Israel. Is that not why Jesus chose twelve of us?

But there is only eleven. That's right, Jesus sent Judas out. Why? Is Judas the betrayer? And Jesus knew it? He sends his betrayer out to betray him… and us? What could Judas be thinking? What could Jesus be thinking?

Everything is working out according to Jesus' plan. When Jesus said that Mary had prepared him for his burial, he was serious. He is planning to die! Then what's with the angels ascending and descending on the Son of Man? Was he mocking me? Have we all been set up?

That cannot be. I know better. No better man has ever lived. No more honest man, no more godly man. He believes that he is the Messiah. I cannot doubt that. He intends our good. I cannot doubt that either. Nor can I doubt his power were he to choose to use it. I have seen too many displays of power. I know that he could call down a legion of angels if he so chose. All the more confusing is this evening.

I am so tired. This is like a bad dream. Maybe that is what it is. Maybe I will wake to find it just that. I have so much wanted to see those angels. I long to look on them. I suppose I will have to wait until the kingdom of God comes. I expected all along that it would come only through battle, even death of followers, but I expected us to be standing beside our Captain in the fight, maybe even alongside angels. It seems in the Teacher's wild plan that the kingdom must come through his own death.

I am so very, very confused and tired.

Malchus

And when those who were around him saw what would follow, they said, "Lord, shall we strike with the sword?" And one of them struck the servant of the high priest and cut off his right ear. But Jesus said, "No more of this!" And he touched his ear and healed him.

—Luke 22:49–51

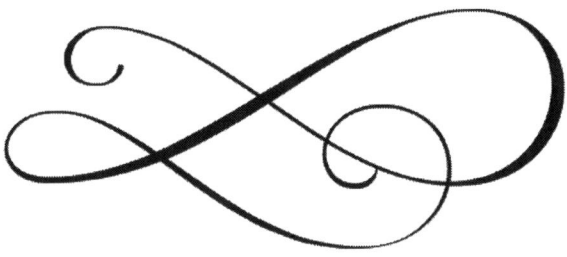

For full story:
Luke 22:47–51; Matthew 26:51–54; John 18:1–11

It was so unexpected; I was caught off guard. We were told that there would be no violent opposition. Judas assured us of it. We were arresting a religious teacher and his disciples, not a leader of a rebellion. These were not Zealots. There would be no weapons, certainly not a sword.

I am the servant of the high priest Caiaphas. He sent me and my cousin to observe the proceedings and report to him. I carried no weapon; perhaps that is why the disciple called Peter felt brave enough to strike at me.

I did not know what to expect on this late-night expedition. We were to arrest the teacher known as Jesus of Nazareth. Needless to say, there was much controversy surrounding him. Reports had started coming in about three years earlier. John, whom they called the Baptist, had been the most recent "prophet" from God. These prophets appear with somewhat regularity. Their message is much the same—we are all wicked and should repent or else prepare for the judgment of God. The judgments of all our previous oppressors down to the present subjection to the Roman Empire apparently are not enough punishment for us. But these prophets are harmless enough, and even John would have been left alone if he had not meddled in Herod's personal affairs.

But Jesus was different. For one thing there were the miraculous healings. The reports of healings came in at a steady rate—all kinds of healings: illnesses cured, lepers cleansed, lame able to walk, deaf able to hear, even blind able to see. And then evil spirits cast out with but a command. My master sent priests to verify these works, and they attested to their reality.

No, Jesus of Nazareth could not be ignored. Besides the healings and exorcisms, word came that he had miraculously fed thousands. Maybe, maybe not, but it took little foresight to see what it was all leading to—the masses would acclaim him to be the Anointed One, the Messiah, the King. We heard that he could still storms and walk on water.

What troubled Caiaphas and his fellow leaders the most were the Nazarene's teachings. Jesus spoke as if God's kingdom had already ushered in a new age. There were warnings of judgment, yes, but even more a call to be living a radically different life in God's kingdom. And it was radical. If he had preached breaking free from the Roman oppression, or even preached that the Roman oppression was the result of sin, that would have been expected. But he spoke almost as if the empire did not exist.

That's probably why he did not get into trouble with the Roman authorities. But he did get the Jewish authorities, led by my master, riled up. They regarded him as heretical and a danger to the Jewish people's welfare. He was quite vocal about the hypocrisy of the Pharisees, but then Caiaphas and most of the priests were Sadducees, who had always regarded that legalistic party as stuck-up hypocrites, as well.

No, my master is more intelligent than those fundamentalists and far more shrewd. He let me in on his thoughts once. "Malchus, your name means 'my king.' That is what this peasant aspires to become. He teaches about a new order, a new kingdom. He doesn't say aloud that he is to be the king of this new order, but mark my words that such is what he intends to become. He will not be satisfied until you and even I address him as 'my King.' Even if the hammer of the Romans does not fall upon him, I can never let such blasphemy take place."

And he did use that word "blasphemy." Caiaphas was suspicious that Jesus' idea of kingship was more than the presumption of a peasant for earthly recognition. This Jesus forgave sins; he referred to the Holy One personally as his father. And the claims grew more audacious. He didn't simply point people the way to the Father; he was the way. He was the door; he was the good shepherd. He almost got stoned at least once for words that came close to equating himself with the Holy One. This is why all of Jesus' miracles were of little account to Caiaphas. For sure, miraculous signs were to accompany the Messiah, but these were not the teachings of the Messiah. They were of a madman, even of the devil.

It all came to a head with the episode of Lazarus. They say Jesus raised him from the dead. That was preposterous, but my master oddly took it seriously and became all the more alarmed. He called his chief priests and even the chief Pharisees together to discuss what to do. I was present when he rose and made his own prophesy: "It is better that one man should die for the people, than that the whole nation should perish. This Jesus of Nazareth will die for the nation of Israel, and his death will lead to the gathering into one the children of God who are scattered abroad."

And so that night I gladly took my master's assignment to accompany the arrest party. If Caiaphas, the High Priest of Israel, said that the Nazarene was a dangerous blasphemer whose death was necessary, then action was needed for sure. Judas came to the house and said all was ready. He then led us up a hillside to an olive garden called Gethsemane. He said that was where Jesus often took his disciples in the evenings. It would be dark, but he would know where to find his master and signal to us by giving Jesus a kiss of greeting.

Again, he assured us that there would be no problem. Jesus was peaceful and his disciples were neither armed nor brave, even if they had known what to do with a weapon. A show of force would scare them away.

All would have gone to plan if that rash disciple had not acted out of control. What was he doing with a sword? Better for it to have been in the hand of a soldier who knew what and what not to do with a weapon than for it to be in the grasp of this reckless fisherman. But he lashed out with it, and where should the blade fall but upon me. I swerved just in time for it to miss getting my head split in two but not enough for my right ear. He cut it clean off.

I fell to my knees as my body went into shock. I grabbed where my ear should have been; blood was flowing out. I began to black out, my hands now in the dirt; then another hand touched me. I felt…what did I feel? I put my hand back up to the bloody spot, only… my ear was there. My mind was still spinning. Voices were dying away when my cousin lifted me up. Just the two of us were in the garden. The arrest party was heading back to my master's house; the Nazarene's followers had apparently fled away.

"What happened?" I asked my cousin.

"Your ear was struck off and Jesus healed you."

"He healed me? How?"

"He picked up your ear off the ground and placed it back on the side of your head."

"What did he say?"

"Nothing to you. He told the guy with the sword to put it away, then something about the Scriptures being fulfilled."

"The Scriptures fulfilled?"

"Yes, and he spoke calmly as though the arrest party had simply joined a teaching time with his disciples."

I went back to my master's house with my cousin and stood where I could observe the proceedings. It went mostly to plan, though the Nazarene confused and troubled my master and the priests and Sanhedrin leaders with his silence. In silence he bore the beatings and mockery; in silence he marched to the Roman procurator's house. In silence he listened to the crowd call for his crucifixion and to Pilate pronounce his sentence of death. In silence he suffered his lashing and walked outside the city to the place of crucifixion. But for a few words, he bore the crucifixion in silence, even as priests sent by Caiaphas mocked him as king, taunting him to come down if God were pleased with him.

What was going on? Why was Jesus not defending himself? Why, he was acting as one of the sheep taken to be... And then it came to me, what Jesus had meant by the Scriptures being fulfilled. They were the words of a true prophet, Isaiah:

> He was oppressed, and he was afflicted,
>   yet he opened not his mouth;
> like a lamb that is led to the slaughter,
>   and like a sheep that before its shearers is silent,
>   so he opened not his mouth.

I looked up at him and confessed, "My King."

Pilate

So when Pilate saw that he was gaining nothing, but rather that a riot was beginning, he took water and washed his hands before the crowd, saying, "I am innocent of this man's blood; see to it yourselves." And all the people answered, "His blood be on us and on our children!" Then he released for them Barabbas, and having scourged Jesus, delivered him to be crucified.

—Matthew 27:24–26

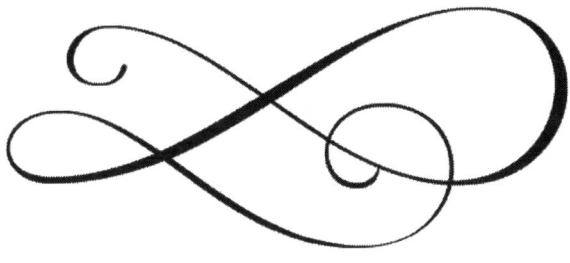

For full story:
John 18:28–19:16; Matthew 27:11–26

I have washed my hands of the whole affair. I am not responsible for that man's death. I made it clear then that I thought him innocent. I will not, I cannot be held accountable for his crucifixion. It was they—the Jewish leaders and the crowd—who convicted him guilty of treason. It was they who demanded his crucifixion.

They had trapped me. How I hate those conniving Jewish leaders and their sanctimonious priests. I hate all the Jews for their fanatical religion. I am a religious man myself. I pay due honor to our Roman gods, but these people are unreasonable. The Roman Empire rules by power, yes, but also by its fair dealings with the nations. We do not destroy nations; we make them better; we civilize them. We are the ones who have created peace among the nations. We let them keep their ways as much as possible. We let them practice their religions. And we have gone overboard to appease this insignificant nation that thinks it is the chosen people of God.

Oh, yes, they have only one god. There are no other gods—only their Yahweh who claims them alone as his holy nation. Such a claim shows the absurdity of their religion. What god would choose this desolate land filled with ignorant, violent natives? I despise them.

All the nations have gods. They have managed to live within the Roman system. They have been adaptable. Not these Jews. They cannot abide us heathens. We are their conquerors! Can they not get that into their heads? We are the rulers! We are not brutish destroyers. We appreciate the good in other nations and cultures, but there is nothing in this god-forsaken land to admire, especially their god-saturated culture.

There was nothing out of the ordinary ordering the likeness of Caesar to be carried on the soldiers' ensigns when they marched into Jerusalem. He is the head of the Roman Empire. No other nation complained. But no, the holy city cannot tolerate graven images. The images were of a man, not a god. No one was being told to worship the images.

But I did want to make a statement of who was in charge. That backfired. The religious leaders (all the leaders are religious leaders) bared their necks when I threatened to behead them. They won that round. What was I to do—cut off all their heads? I would have had a mess on my hands from the insurrectionists and my authorities above me. I showed what stern stuff I was made of later when they in their insolence protested my appropriating temple funds for a water project. Some bludgeoned heads quelled that little protestation. The blood of Galilean pilgrims mingled with their sacrifices? I had to deal with another band of rebellious Jews using their pilgrimage as an excuse to defy moderate Roman law. We did not mix their blood with the blood of their sacrifices. How could we when we were restricted from entering their sacrificial court?

That is the galling part of it all. The Jews placed restrictions on their Roman rulers! The authorities above me let them get away with it, when we should have crushed their rebellious ways from the beginning. I should never have been placed in my humiliating predicament that early morning.

Jewish leaders wanted to see me. They had a prisoner that needed my attention. I had to go out to them so that they would not defile their holy feet for their Passover feast. The Passover was the reason I was in Jerusalem. I had to be there with an extra contingency of soldiers. Passover recalls their being set free from another empire. Imagine then the mischief such a celebration stirs up.

They had an insurgent on their hands—someone proclaiming himself their Christ, the King of the Jews. I smelled a rat. For all their hypocrisy, they had never betrayed an insurrectionist before. Why this man? What trouble were they trying to get me into this time?

I brought him inside and questioned him. His name was Jesus. I had heard of him. He was harmless. Never spoke against Rome. Indeed, word was that he was teaching the Jews to go the extra mile in responding to us—hardly insurrectionist material.

I was ready to let him go free, if only to spite these leaders. But he would not cooperate. "Are you King of the Jews?" I asked. "You have said so." What kind of answer was that? I asked again. He replied, "Do you say this of your own accord, or did others say it to you about me?" I was not the one to be interrogated. I was not the prisoner; I was the judge. "Am I a Jew? Your own nation and the chief priests have delivered you over to me. What have you done?"

Give me some cooperation. I knew the charges were trumped up. All I wanted was for him to level with me. But he goes into this speech about his kingdom being of another world. What was he talking about? So he was claiming to be a king, I noted. Then he hits me with that irritating line again—"You have said so." I was about to rebuke him for being impertinent, when he goes into another strange declaration: "For this purpose I was born and for this purpose I have come into the world—to bear witness to the truth. Everyone who is of the truth listens to my voice."

"What is truth?" I scoffed. Truth is I didn't know what to say. Who was this man standing calmly with his life in my hands and talking to me as a teacher to a student. I walked out. Whoever he was, he did not deserve death. I am not the ruthless, bloodthirsty tyrant the Jews have made me out to be. If I used an iron rod, it was to put down the rebellious; this man was no rebel.

I went out to reason with the leaders. They were hardened and determined to be rid of this Jesus. "He purports to be our king," they kept throwing at me. "That is treason. We have no king but Caesar." Ha, that is exactly what the Jews will not consent to and here are these malevolent holy men turning the tables against me. "If you release this man, you are not Caesar's friend." I tried everything—I had him scourged; I appealed straight to the crowd that was gathering; I even offered to release him against the option of the notorious Barabbas, but somehow the leaders had whipped them up. They wanted Jesus dead. "Crucify him! We have no king but Caesar!"

What could I have done? Complaints about me had been made before, and now for Caesar to hear from Jewish leaders that I would not punish a man presenting himself as King of the Jews? If all this was not enough, I get a message from my wife to have nothing to do with this man because of a dream. A dream! But the gods do speak through dreams.

Very well, then, I would have nothing to do with him. I called for a bowl of water, and in the presence of all declared myself innocent of this man's blood. They want him dead? Very well, then, his blood would be on their heads, not mine. I let him go. Yes, yes, I delivered him over to my soldiers for crucifixion, but I was forced into carrying out their will.

I had been tricked. I am not an unjust man. I am just one Roman official trying to do my duty and keep peace. Maybe I could have done more, but Jesus was being obstinate himself. He would say nothing in front of the leaders, nothing in front of the crowd. You'd think he wanted to be crucified.

"Everyone who is of the truth listens to my voice." I did not have time to listen. His enemies were calling for his blood. They were calling for me to shed his blood. Didn't he understand that? Didn't he understand my power? Power was the very thing he denied I had. I would have condemned him for such a flippant remark alone, except that he spoke, it seemed, from pity rather than from arrogance.

No, I am not an unjust man. My hands are innocent. I did what any reasonable person in my position would have done. I could not give up my own life, which is what I might have been doing if I had stood by him. He may have been an innocent man, but he was nothing more than a man. I had the sign, "King of the Jews," placed over his head to note the reason for the execution and, I will admit, to thumb my nose at my manipulators. Was Jesus king? Of course not; there is no king but Caesar.

Simon of Cyrene

And they led him out to crucify him. And they compelled a passerby, Simon of Cyrene, who was coming in from the country, the father of Alexander and Rufus, to carry his cross. And they brought him to the place called Golgotha (which means Place of a Skull).

—Mark 15:20–22

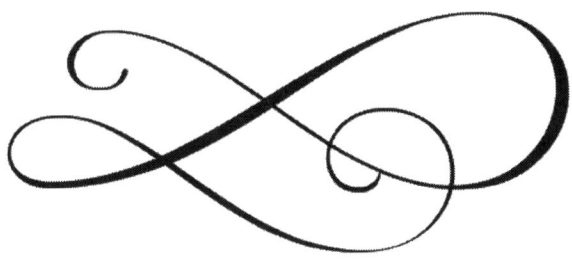

For full story:
Mark 15:16–22

I come from Cyrene. My family has lived in that great city of North Africa for many generations. They were among the first of the Diaspora, the dispersion of Jewish people around the Mediterranean. Though my ancestors were forced to settle there, they soon enough embraced their new home and even invited others of the Jewish nation to come and make the city their home. We have always been allowed to practice our religion and were faithful to make pilgrimages to Jerusalem for the feast days.

That is why I was in Jerusalem and was just making it in time for the Passover. I knew something was up as I neared the entrance of the city. Jerusalem is always crowded and noisy during the Passover, but the commotion was greater, and this time I could see a group of soldiers. I entered through the gate. Up ahead there appeared to be some kind of parade. The guards were pushing people back to make way for something. I worked my way to the edge of the crowd. I could see now. The soldiers were leading prisoners—prisoners who were carrying beams of wood. Then I understood. Poor creatures—they were being led to their crucifixion.

They must have been Zealots, insurrectionists. Why else crucifixion? The Passover is the time they can be expected to do something stupid. Still, one cannot help but pity them. They had already been beaten. They were filthy, dressed in rags. One in particular was most miserable. I shuddered then at the thought of being in his place. He barely had life in him, he had been beaten so terribly. Even with a tunic on, I could tell that the skin on his back had been shredded. It was a wonder he could walk at all, much less bear a heavy beam. Even so, he stumbled right in front of me.

I had seen enough. I was about to slip back through the crowd, when a soldier grabbed my arm. "You, pick up that beam!" Was he joking? I tried to pull my arm away, but he held it tightly and then thrust me forward, forward into the nightmare.

This couldn't be happening. The soldiers and the other prisoners had stopped. The crowd, or mob, I should say, were shouting. I thought I heard curses and also wailings. Some were shaking their fists and others were crying. Noise all about me. The soldier pushed me again, threatening me with his whip. I looked at the wretched victim who was kneeling on all fours. I did not want to feel that whip.

I picked up one end of the beam lying on the dusty road. Two soldiers roughly lifted the victim onto his feet. One cracked his whip as a driver of beasts would do. The victim passed by me, looking in my eyes with his own sad eyes. And then I followed, balancing the beam on one shoulder. No wonder he had stumbled. The weight was heavy enough for a sound man.

I could handle the burden of the weight. The greater burden, the onerous part of it all was the humiliation. I am a free citizen, and I was being treated as a slave. And publicly—before a massive crowd lining the road out of Jerusalem. I came to the Passover to celebrate the freedom of my people, not its slavery! And then, to be pressed into such ignoble service. I knew the practice of Roman soldiers forcing the citizens of conquered nations to carry their packs up to a mile. But this was the cross of a thief, of an insurrectionist, maybe a murderer. I was carrying the cross beam in his place! How shameful. How humiliating.

The crowd would not let up. They lined the road the entire way to Golgotha, cursing and crying and taunting. It was hot enough; the close crowd made the air suffocating. The pace was agonizingly slow. The two victims with their crosses struggled, and though he no longer had his burden, it was obvious that the most wretched of the three was struggling to stay on his feet. It seemed that the focus was mostly on him.

I looked at him. There was nothing remarkable about him. He seemed like any other man, any other wretched man. Blood dripped below his tunic and from his marred face. What had he done that led him to such an end?

Suddenly he stopped. A group of women were mourning and lamenting. I assumed they were weeping for all three of the victims, but he acted as though it was all for him. His response confirmed for me that he was an insurrectionist, as I had first surmised. "Daughters of Jerusalem, do not weep for me, but weep for yourselves and for your children." Then he predicted the destruction to come. Yes, just like a martyr prophesying doom.

The soldiers pushed him on. Now I was angry. I was carrying the beam of a cross for a fool. My ears picked up some of the taunts being directed at this fool. "Save yourself, King of the Jews!" "Hail the King of Israel!" So that is what he had purported to be. No wonder they were cursing and mocking him. I wondered if he had had many followers, and all the more my own humiliation bore down on me—here I was his only follower bearing his cross.

He turned his head, looked at me, and then ahead again. His eyes were filled with grief, and yet, what was it? What was it in that brief glance? There was grief but not the despair and the anger that were in the faces of the other two victims. On that face was pure, untainted sorrow. Ever since his crazy words to the women, he had remained silent as he was led to his execution. I wanted to be angry but all I could feel was pity. I was following the man of sorrows.

Another taunt. "You saved others; you cannot save yourself." He saved others? Saved them from what? What could this man, cursed of God, save anyone from? I followed and I listened. Not all the voices were of mockers. There were loving voices calling this peasant, "Rabbi" and even "my Lord." Were they his followers? They did not sound like Zealots. What did he save them from?

I heard a name. Someone called him Jesus. Yes, someone else said it—Jesus of Nazareth. I had heard of him, even as far as Cyrene. He was the miracle-worker. This bloody, staggering wretch was the miracle-working prophet that some had even believed might be the Messiah. I was following Jesus the Christ. I laughed bitterly within. Some Messiah and some follower he was left with.

His end was near, the end of his journey to the cross, that is. He still had a long tortured death to bear, and for what? For whom? I began to feel despair. This Jesus had no doubt been a good man, misguided as he might be. But whatever good he might have done, whatever saving he might have done and hoped to do, it only led to an ignoble death. I was following a lamb led to slaughter.

The crossbeam seemed to grow heavier on my shoulder. I was glad when we reached the journey's end and could lay it down and to have nothing more to do with this travesty and this poor wretch. As I rested, the soldiers quickly, efficiently nailed him to the cross and hoisted it up. I stared despondently at him, then turned to go when I heard Jesus speak: "Father, forgive them, for they know not what they do."

I could not leave then. I stayed and watched it all, heard it all. I watched the agony, the mockery, the callousness, the weeping and grief. The sun darkened; the victim cried out in thirst, in pain, in abandonment, and then (how could it be?) even in trust as an offering to his heavenly Father, and finally, as though he was bringing his own life to its finish.

I returned to the city with much to think about. Who was it that I had followed? Whose cross did I bear? I had to know. A hand touched my shoulder, and a voice whispered, "Follow me." It turned out to be the voice of a follower of Jesus—a disciple he was called. He led me to where others had gathered in hiding. He had seen me bear the cross of his master, and they all seemed grateful for the service I had rendered. I stayed with them for three days listening to their stories, when on the third day…well, you know what happened that third day. I determined then that for the rest of my life I would deny myself, take up my cross, and follow Jesus.

The Centurion at the Cross

And Jesus uttered a loud cry and breathed his last. And the curtain of the temple was torn in two, from top to bottom. And when the centurion, who stood facing him, saw that in this way he breathed his last, he said, "Truly this man was the Son of God!"

—Mark 15:37–39

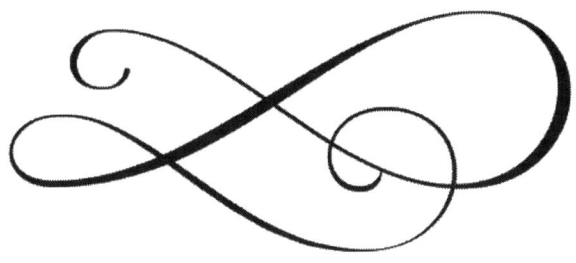

For full story:
Mark 15:33–39; Luke 23:32–47

The tedium—it is the tedium that is most difficult to bear. I know it sounds crass, but after more than a hundred crucifixions, one tends to become benumbed of the suffering and even contemptuous of the victims. How else can a soldier carry out such debased work?

I was trained to be a soldier, a warrior in battle, an enforcer of the law. I signed up to fight for the empire—to win victory over Rome's enemies and to extend her rule over barbaric lands. I earned my position by courage and leadership, and with the authority now over one hundred soldiers, I looked for the opportunity of greater glory to lead my men in battle and to establish order in hostile lands.

I relished the difficult assignment. I embraced my orders to serve in this hostile land of rebels, of this outpost filled with religious zealotry that defied Roman authority. Here was a place to prove my own mettle. I had fought barbarians and knew—or thought I knew—how to fight against these Jewish rebels.

At first things went as I expected. My legion attacked a stronghold of Zealots, as they are called, in the hills. We defeated them easily, and those not killed in battle we crucified on crosses lining the road leading into Jerusalem. That was a message for any others contemplating rebellion against Rome.

There were no more outbreaks—no attacking rebel bands. No, something less definable, more insidious. There was the knife cutting the throat of a lax soldier, the quiet murder of a Jewish "traitor," a tax collector, one of our suspected spies. We caught perpetrators. Judgment was swift and the punishment invariably crucifixion. Surely the lesson would be learned, but the acts of terrorism only grew, so much so that crucifixion became almost a daily event, a daily grind. I became nothing more than a glorified executioner of a slow, tedious killing process.

The Centurion at the Cross

Whoever the victim might be, he died the same. Eventually his spirit would break, and he would die cursing—cursing us, cursing his people, cursing his god. Oh yes, that was the most galling part of it all for them—that their god abandoned them. They had been fighting his cause, fighting for his people. They had joined the cause to rid the land of infidel oppressors; they had fought to restore the kingdom of God. And now here they were, nailed to a cross in humiliation, in excruciating agony. No heroics now. They wept, they begged for death; they screamed in pain and anguish. Their god had abandoned them.

Jesus of Nazareth—another messiah to crucify. There was some difference. He certainly did not have much of a following. The best I could tell was that the Jewish leaders had a grudge against him. There was little to see in him. He did not speak, much less rail against the heathen Romans. No, he did not speak at all. He seemed resigned to his fate. Even as we scourged him and handled him, well, roughly, he endured it stoically.

We drove him and two other criminals outside the city to the site. My men worked efficiently. Quickly we drove the nails and lifted the cross.

"Father, forgive them, for they know not what they do."

I had become somewhat proficient in understanding their language, but did I misunderstand? I asked a Jew nearby to confirm what he had said. Yes, he had asked that we be forgiven. Really? To be forgiven? We did not know what we were doing?

We had a clear idea what we were doing. We were crucifying another… well, to tell the truth none of us knew who or what he was. He evidently claimed to be a king. We knew he had followers claiming him to be some kind of messiah. But what had he actually done? We never received reports of this Jesus of Nazareth trying to foment rebellion. There was no record of him inciting violence. We never heard of him speaking ill of us. He seemed rather harmless.

And here he was hanging on a cross that we nailed him to, and he was praying to his god to forgive us. Everyone else had prayed to this Jewish god, as well. They prayed for him to strike us dead. They prayed for him to display his wrath against us heathen. Forgive us? What a funny thing to say.

And he called his god, Father. That was a new one for me. I had heard Yahweh, God of Hosts, Holy One, and other titles that supposedly were to overawe us. "Father" I had never heard. Did he think he was a son of a god? We have sons and daughters of gods in our pantheon—Hercules, son of Zeus, is the most respected demigod among us soldiers. But I never heard of a Jew speaking that way.

Forgive us? What a silly thing to say. I knew it wouldn't be long, though, before the curses came.

Curses soon came but from the onlookers, and not directed toward us but toward him! They were mocking him. The dignified religious leaders were mocking him! What had he done to make them sink into degrading behavior? My own men joined in the fun, but they did that as much to fight the tedium and to insulate themselves against the horror they had to participate in. It was not personal, not like it was for these enemies of his. My goodness, even the other two victims joined in. One did change in the end, though. I could not hear clearly, but he seemed to have made his peace with this Jesus. I don't know what changed him unless it was watching the way Jesus endured his suffering and the mockery. Everyone was goading him about saving himself.

"He saved others; he cannot save himself."

"He is the King of Israel; let him come down now from the cross, and we will believe in him."

And there was one that was the most galling: "He trusts in God; let God deliver him now, if he desires him. For he said, 'I am the Son of God.'"

So he did think he was a son of God. Did he think his Father was about to save him? Many other victims had died despairing the deliverance they had cried out for.

But he ignored them all, and his first words were to his mother, whom we had let come near. All of the pain and anguish he was enduring, and he thought of providing for his mother. Sweet, but I knew what the torment of the cross would bring him to.

The hours trudged on. The torment built. But something unnerving was also happening—darkness covering the land. I had seen storms, had been caught in sudden storms, but this was no mere cloud covering. It was as if the sun itself had been eclipsed. And as that darkness fell upon us, I heard the words I had been waiting to hear: "My God, my God, why have you forsaken me!" Some fools thought he was calling out for Elijah, but I had heard these words before from the lips of other devoted victims. I even knew that he was quoting their sacred Scriptures. A rabbi had explained the cry of despair to me. This was the true horror of all the victims. The god they had believed in, whom they had fought for, who they believed would deliver them right up to the cross—their god had abandoned them. What they had believed in was nothing but a lie.

"I thirst."

I knew he did. How he could even speak, I don't know. What I expected now was the weeping, the raging, and soon—it had to be soon—the cursing. Curse God. They all did in the end.

But the curse never came. After he was given some wine from a sponge, he cried out, "It is finished." I wasn't sure what he meant except, perhaps, that he was finished, defeated at last. It certainly seemed that way, and yet somehow he found the strength to call out one last time. Would this be the curse?

"Father, into your hands I commit my spirit!"

Father? He called the god who had abandoned him, Father? He commits himself into this Father's hands? I was there, standing in front of him. I know what he said. I know the agony; I know the despair; I know what ought to have happened; I know the curses that ought to have come from his lips, but he died trusting in God, his Father. He had the trust that only a son can have, the dignity that only the Son of God can possess.

I will not rest until I find the truth about him. I am through with nailing men to crosses. I want to know what this man, this Son of God was doing on that cross.

John
after the Crucifixion

Standing by the cross of Jesus were his mother and his mother's sister, Mary the wife of Clopas, and Mary Magdalene. When Jesus saw his mother and the disciple whom he loved standing nearby, he said to his mother, "Woman, behold, your son!" Then he said to the disciple, "Behold, your mother!" And from that hour the disciple took her to his own home.

—John 19:25–27

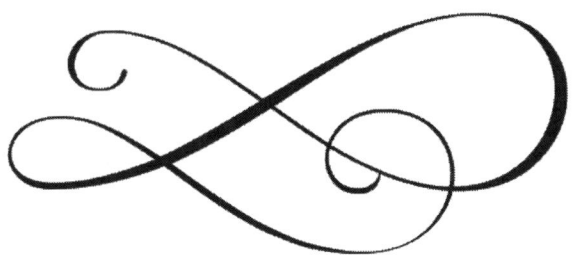

For full story:
John 19:16–37

I must keep my head. I cannot break down. Not now. My Master gave me responsibility to care for his mother. I cannot let him down.

I am tired. I have had little sleep. The small bit I had last night shames me. And what I have had to witness weighs me down with grief. I don't know if I can go on. I don't know what to do. But I must take care of Mary. I cannot let my Master down.

Where is Peter? James returned to the house after the arrest. Andrew and Philip have recently come in. Perhaps the others will come back shamefacedly like them. We are all ashamed, all grieved, all scared, all in despair. But I cannot give in, not now. With Peter gone, I must show strength.

I ran away with the others though not far. Peter and I were together. We carefully followed the soldiers to the high priest's house. My family has distant connection with his family, and I was able to get us both inside the courtyard. I determined to enter the house, but Peter held back. I have not seen him since. Where is he?

Others are slipping back in now. I expect everyone soon, other than Judas. What happened to Judas? Why would he do such a thing? But Teacher knew all along. He said at supper that one of us would betray him. Yes, Teacher knew. He knew everything that would happen. He had said more than once that he would be betrayed and suffer and be crucified. He was trying to prepare us last night for his departure.

What did he say? I must remember. I have got to remember if I am to go on. He talked as if he were going away on a journey. Yes, he was going back to his Father's house. The temple? No, it couldn't be that. Heaven? Is that what he meant? He said he would come back, but how? His responses only confused us more.

John after the Crucifixion

Inside the high priest's house, I found a corner in the assembly room. It looked like most of the Sanhedrin had gathered. Some were still hurrying in. The meeting must have been planned. I looked at my Lord. He stood calm, far different from the anxiety he had shown in the garden before the arrest. It was that calmness at his arrest that had most bewildered us. "Shall I not drink the cup that the Father has given me?" he had said to Peter.

Those words haunt me now. Obsessed with our own glory, my brother and I had foolishly asked Teacher to give us the two most honored chairs in his kingdom. He asked then if we could drink the same cup that he would, and we—the braggards we are—boasted that we could. I kept hidden in that corner as my Lord fended off questions about his disciples.

Witnesses were brought forward accusing him of some absurd charge about threatening to tear down the temple, but their testimonies did not square up with each other. Some other charges and challenges were thrown about. They were trying to trip Teacher up, make him incriminate himself, but he would not speak. I think what aggravated them more was his calmness. He could not be intimidated.

Finally, the high priest solemnly charged him to answer the question, "Are you the Messiah, the Son of the Blessed?" The two stared at each other. "I am, and you will see the Son of Man seated at the right hand of the Power and coming on the clouds of heaven." These dignified leaders lost it then. The room went into an uproar as the verdict of blasphemy was pronounced. They tore their robes. Some went up to him and spat in his face. Some slapped him and mocked him. I kept in my corner.

They took him out of the room. I learned that he was to be taken to the procurator's headquarters. I slipped out into the courtyard. Peter was not there. Where is he? I would have to watch this horror unfold alone.

Alone. He said that we would scatter and leave him to face his fate alone. But then, he would not be alone, he said. His Father is with him. Father, I need you now with me.

He also said he would send the Helper, the Holy Spirit. I don't quite understand. He said that he had to go away just so that this Helper would come. I would rather have my Lord. What can this Helper do? How can he replace our Lord?

It was in the court area of the praetorium that I saw Jesus' mother, Mary. His sister and Mary Magdalene was with her. They had heard about the arrest from James. We could not hear what the high priest and delegation were saying to Procurator Pilate. He went inside with Jesus. When he came back out, we could then hear him. He found no guilt. And then he spoke to all of us. "You have the custom that I release one prisoner for you at the Passover. I bring out Barabbas and Jesus your king. Who do you choose?"

Barabbas? He was feared by everyone for the insurrection he had led, even more for his reputation as an assassin. Pilate must have been trying to outmaneuver the chief priests. We four called out "Jesus," but to our dismay our voices were drowned out by the call for Barabbas. How could this be? We looked about us and received evil stares.

Pilate was clearly unsettled. He took Jesus back in. When they came back out, we were horrified. Our Lord had been scourged. He could barely stand. Blood was dripping down his face from a crown of thorns on his head. He was dressed in a purple robe. The soldiers had made a mockery of him.

"Crucify him!" The whole crowd was shouting. Why had they turned against him?

"He is your king!" Pilate said.

"We have no king but Caesar."

This clearly unnerved Pilate. He turned Teacher over to the soldiers for crucifixion. Mary screamed in horror. We steadied her and led her away from the crowd. We tried to take her home, but she refused. She must be with her son. And so we followed the train of soldiers out the city to Golgotha. We took our place near the foot of the cross for every cruel minute.

How did this happen? How could my Master be hanging on a cross? What will happen to us? Jesus told us to expect to be next, that we will be hated and persecuted. Are our enemies searching for us now? What would we say if brought to trial like our Master? I don't see how I can face crucifixion, not after what I have witnessed.

How could the soldiers be so callous? They cast lots for Teacher's clothing. And then came the mockery from the chief priests and others about saving himself. What is wrong with everyone? Why such hatred? Is there to be no show of compassion?

"Woman, behold, your son." I looked up at my Lord. He was speaking to us. He looked at me. "Behold, your mother." The compassion came from the cross, the compassion of a son for his mother. I understood. I promised him then that I would take care of his mother.

But can I? Can I even take care of myself? My Master is gone, crucified as a cursed slave. We few disciples and women are left alone in the midst of enemies.

"In me you may have peace. In the world you will have tribulation. But take heart; I have overcome the world."

How could Teacher speak of overcoming the world when the world nailed him on a cross? It is Rome that has overcome the world, and our enemies have overcome our Lord. And yet, he knew what would happen. How could he see crucifixion and speak of victory? How could he see death and speak of life?

But life is what he saw at the end. "The hour has come for the Son of Man to be glorified. Truly, truly, I say to you, unless a grain of wheat falls into the earth and dies, it remains alone; but if it dies, it bears much fruit."

The hour has passed. Teacher lies in a tomb. We disciples hide. It is in this hour that I know he wants me to believe that somehow his life, even his death, has not been in vain. It is in this hour that he wants his followers to keep together as one. I must wait for that Helper to come. I must wait for the light to overcome the darkness, for life to come out of death.

Joseph of Arimathea

When it was evening, there came a rich man from Arimathea, named Joseph, who also was a disciple of Jesus. He went to Pilate and asked for the body of Jesus. Then Pilate ordered it to be given to him. And Joseph took the body and wrapped it in a clean linen shroud and laid it in his own new tomb…

—Matthew 27:57–60

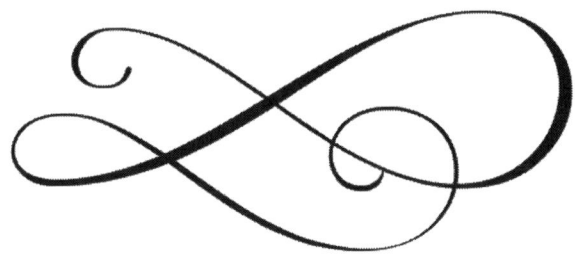

For full story:
Matthew 27:57–60; John 19:38–42

I had to do something. I was ashamed, ashamed that I had not owned up to believing that he was the Messiah. So why now, when it is clear that he is not the One for whom we hope, do I come forth to show my devotion?

It seemed like the decent thing to do. The Romans would have thrown his body into a common grave, maybe not even that. They would have defiled Jesus' body. And yet how much more could it have been defiled than it already was to be hanged on a tree—a curse to the Romans and even by our law a curse to God?

Why now? Why not before when I first believed he was the Anointed One? Why not then profess my faith in him?

I can explain why not before. I am a man of responsibility. I am a member of the Sanhedrin, the highest council of my people. My actions have consequences. What if I was wrong about Jesus and led people astray? That is why my brothers on the council and the priests were so careful. There had been others who had professed to be sent from God, if not the Messiah himself. Some had drawn many followers. They all perished and their followers suffered. No, when you have responsibility, you cannot follow your whims.

And so we sent messengers to observe him and to ask him questions. He was drawing crowds, mostly through his signs of wonder. Even I was sent out to observe and to make a report. I saw with my own eyes his signs. I saw the sick healed, even the blind given sight. I saw certified lepers be cleansed. If someone truly is from God, signs will accompany him that certify his claim. I could not deny these signs of Jesus of Nazareth.

Then there were his teachings. He spoke of the kingdom of God, and with authority. He spoke in such a way that one felt his words piercing one's heart—as the old expression says it, dividing bone and marrow. I am a life-long student of the Scriptures, but here was an untrained man taking those Scriptures I thought I knew so well and turning them back so as to shine into my very heart. And I did not like what I saw—the meanness of spirit, the hypocrisy, and too many other sins. No, I did not like such teaching, and yet I knew his words to be true.

Then there were his claims about himself. He was careful with his words, but my training gave me ears to hear what he was saying beneath the surface. He thought he was the Messiah. That was clear enough. And I came to believe him. I believed he was the One to usher in the kingdom of God.

So why not confess him then? I was the only Sanhedrin member besides Nicodemus. We consulted with each other. We thought it best to wait. Jesus himself was careful with his words. When he publicly declared himself, we would then stand up for him. There was too much opposition from the leadership, and to step out now might harm Jesus' plans. No doubt he had a strategy. It was best for us to wait. At the right time, wait for the right time. We would be there for him then.

The right time never came. Plans were made behind our backs by our leaders. We were summoned the very night before Passover to try Jesus of Nazareth. We protested. We pointed out the impropriety of meeting at night and other violations of the proceedings. The trial was highly irregular. Be sure we pointed that out very clearly.

What more could we have done? Speak up for him? We did in our own way. But he would not speak up for himself! He was on trial for his life and he would not speak. He was asked directly if he were the Messiah. Even then his words were ambiguous, and only by the decree of the high priest was he declared guilty of blasphemy. We started to protest, but our voices were lost in the shouts of the others condemning him. By that time we knew the cause was lost.

Perhaps, though, that was what Jesus was waiting for. Perhaps now would be the time that he demonstrated who he was. But he remained silent and no sign appeared from heaven, even as he was spat upon and struck.

What went wrong? If he were the Messiah, how could he have let this happen? How could the Holy One let this happen to his Anointed? If I had not known better, I would have thought Jesus had actually planned his death.

I knew his cause was lost when they sent him to Pilate. It was plain that the leaders were orchestrating the proceedings. Pilate would acquiesce. Nicodemus and I heard the sentence given; then we departed. I went to my home, and yet, I could not stay. I was restless. I could not get Jesus off of my mind.

I walked to the site where he was being crucified. He was not the Messiah, no, but he was a good man. He should not die this way. I became aware of someone standing beside me. It was Nicodemus. He too could not stay away. We watched in silence until Nicodemus asked, "What will happen to the body?" I had not thought about it, though we both knew. It would be dumped in an open pit most likely. We looked at each other and understood. This should not happen. We had failed to save his life from desecration; could we not save his body? We had failed because…because we had been too cowardly to act. All of our excuses were rational, reasonable. And they were false. We had failed to confess Jesus publicly because we feared the consequences—our reputations, our standing among our brothers. We had failed.

It was too late now to speak up for Jesus, certainly too late to proclaim him as the Messiah. But there was one last act that we could accomplish if we acted with haste. They would not leave the bodies past sunset because of the Passover. They would do something to kill the victims. We needed to act quickly. Nicodemus already had the necessary spices and materials. I would go to Pilate.

He would see me because of my standing that I have valued so highly. I would now lay it down for this request. I hurried to his house. He came out.

"I have come to ask for the body of Jesus of Nazareth."

He looked at me with incredulity. A member of the Sanhedrin wanting the body? For what purpose? For burial. He seemed surprised that Jesus should have died so quickly. He sent off for a report and went back into the house. The messenger returned with the report that Jesus was dead. Pilate looked at me with a wry smile.

"You may have your body."

I rushed to the site. My servants were waiting for me. I had sent for them while waiting for Pilate's decision. We had not much time before the sun would set. Hurriedly, we lowered his body onto a pallet the servants had brought. Nicodemus came up with his servants.

"Where do we have time to prepare the body and bury him?" Nicodemus asked.

"I know the spot. It is my own grave. Come, it is nearby."

I had bought the site only recently for my family burial. We carried his body and prepared it, wrapping it in layers and spreading the spices and ointments between. The sun was just setting as we laid the body in the cave and rolled the stone over the entrance.

We will hear from our leaders about what we have done, yet, for the first time, I am not worried. As Jesus himself once said, "Do not fear those who kill the body, and after that have nothing more that they can do. But I will warn you whom to fear: fear him who, after he has killed, has authority to cast into hell." When you get that straight—who to fear and who not to fear—decisions become easier to make. This was right to do. We did not show Jesus the proper honor in his life, but we could now show him honor in his death.

I can face whatever the world brings my way, knowing that I have done right before my God. I have heard that the leaders have set guard over the grave site, fearing that the disciples might steal the body. It is reported that Jesus claimed he would rise in three days. Have Nicodemus and I spooked them with our act? It would be nice to think so. Now a resurrection—that would indeed be a sign of wonder.

Nicodemus

Now there was a man of the Pharisees named Nicodemus, a ruler of the Jews. This man came to Jesus by night and said to him, "Rabbi, we know that you are a teacher come from God, for no one can do these signs that you do unless God is with him." Jesus answered him, "Truly, truly, I say to you, unless one is born again he cannot see the kingdom of God."

—John 3:1–3

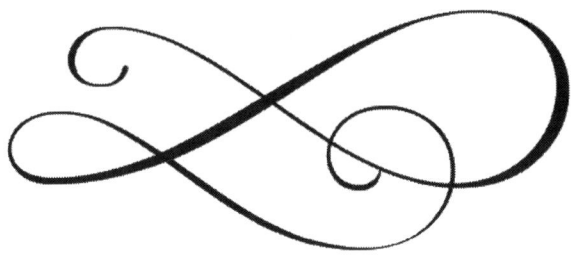

For full story:
John 3:1–15; 19:38–42

Rabbi, we know that you are a teacher come from God, for no one can do these signs that you do unless God is with him.

We placed the Rabbi in the antechamber and proceeded to clean the body.

Truly, truly, I say to you, unless one is born again he cannot see the kingdom of God.

Needless to say, his flesh was covered in blood. It was difficult to clean the holes from the nails and the spear. We then began the wrapping. I had brought myrrh and aloe to glue the linen together and to the body. We began at the feet wrapping each strip of linen, moving to the chest. Strip by strip, layer by layer we covered his lifeless body up to his armpits.

How can a man be born when he is old? Can he enter a second time into his mother's womb and be born?

We then placed his arms to his sides and wrapped them as well, applying the gummy mixture to each layer.

Truly, truly, I say to you, unless one is born of water and the Spirit, he cannot enter the kingdom of God. That which is born of the flesh is flesh, and that which is born of the Spirit is spirit.

We wrapped his head with a cloth, then moved the body into the inner cave and placed it in the niche that Joseph had prepared for himself.

Do not marvel that I said to you, "You must be born again."

We walked out and with the help of the servants we rolled the stone over the opening.

The wind blows where it wishes, and you hear its sound, but you do not know where it comes from or where it goes. So it is with everyone who is born of the Spirit.

The wind had picked up. It was a cold walk home.

How can these things be?

Are you the teacher of Israel and yet you do not understand these things?

All I understood now was that the Rabbi was dead, sealed in a tomb.

Truly, truly, I say to you, we speak of what we know, and bear witness to what we have seen, but you do not receive our testimony. If I have told you earthly things and you do not believe, how can you believe if I tell you heavenly things?

What is there to believe now? Will that crucified body be born again? Is there spirit in that dead flesh?

No one has ascended into heaven except he who descended from heaven, the Son of Man.

May the Holy One be merciful and receive his spirit into paradise. But will he? His signs had indicated that God was with him. Yet, how then could he cry out, "My God, my God, why have you abandoned me?"

The Rabbi hung on a tree. According to Moses, was he not then cursed? How could he have ended on a cross if he were blessed of God?

But then, again, there were the signs. How could he have healed and cast out demons if not from God? How could he have raised Lazarus from the dead?

I agreed with the officers sent once by my brothers to arrest Jesus. They came back without him, and when asked why, replied, "No one ever spoke like this man!" No, no one had. Jesus spoke with authority, not like me and my fellow teachers of the law. None of us spoke with his authority, none of us with his insight, none of us with his courage.

But then, none so mysteriously. Born again? What did he mean? I wanted to understand. That was why I was there risking my reputation as a respectable Pharisee. I was there to give him a hearing and to learn what he was about. That is what I counseled my fellow Pharisees to do before they so readily judged him.

I continued to keep up with the Rabbi, sometimes in the crowd listening to him, more often hearing reports. I studied the Scriptures, and I compared notes with Joseph. His teachings, his signs—they were adding up. We became in our own way followers of Jesus, believing he could be the Messiah. Secretly, of course. We could not be fully certain, and our brother Pharisees became increasingly hostile to him and any known followers.

Hope grew in my heart. Would the Holy One be so merciful as to give me the blessed opportunity of seeing the long-awaited Anointed? Would I see the kingdom restored in all its glory?

Hope still remained at the trial when Caiaphas charged him to answer the question, "Are you the Messiah the Son of the Blessed?" A charge ran through me when Jesus answered, "I am, and you will see the Son of Man seated at the right hand of Power and coming with the clouds of heaven."

Was this the moment? Would he ascend now before our very eyes? Would he bring in his kingdom with power and glory?

It is a dark night following a dark day. I am ready to be home. And yet, how will I be able to sleep? The image of his bloody body lying on the stone table; the image of his dead body wrapped in a shroud. Worst of all, the image of his suffering body lifted up on that cross.

Lifted up? What was it the Rabbi told me that night? I remember now. "As Moses lifted up the serpent in the wilderness, so must the Son of Man be lifted up, that whoever believes in him may have eternal life."

"As Moses lifted up the serpent." Think, Nicodemus, think.

"Are you the teacher of Israel and yet you do not understand these things?" I thought I understood a lot until this Rabbi entered my world.

"As Moses lifted up the serpent." Why did Moses lift that serpent on the pole? The people had been poisoned by serpents. They were dying. Looking at that sign would save them, if they looked on with faith.

It made no sense—looking at the sign of death would save them from death? And yet, through such a foolish sign the power of God to save was displayed. Whoever believed in that foolish sign would have life.

"So must the Son of Man be lifted up." On the cross? Looking at the Messiah hanging on the cross brings life? It is as strange as being born again! What folly! Hanging on a tree is a cursed image. But is it more foolish than looking at a cursed snake? What was happening on that cross? Was it more than a defeated Rabbi dying in defeat?

What was it that the prophet said?

> Surely he has borne our griefs
>   and carried our sorrows;
> yet we esteemed him stricken,
>   smitten by God, and afflicted.
> But he was pierced for our transgressions;
>   he was crushed for our iniquities;
> upon him was the chastisement that brought us peace,
>   and with his wounds we are healed.
> All we like sheep have gone astray;
>   we have turned—every one—to his own way;
> and the Lord has laid on him
>   the iniquity of us all.

The cross! Jesus hanging on the cross is the Suffering Servant? I beheld the iniquity of me and of my people being laid upon him? The Rabbi meant to go to the cross all along. He meant to bear the curse—to bear the curse for us. Instead of death we are to receive life.

But how can I be sure? How can I know that such a sacrifice was accepted by the Holy One? Jesus lies in a tomb. I have wrapped the body and rolled the stone in front of it. What must happen next?

It remains as mysterious to me as being born again.

PART FOUR

HE WAS RAISED

The Angel at the Tomb

Now after the Sabbath, toward the dawn of the first day of the week, Mary Magdalene and the other Mary went to see the tomb. And behold, there was a great earthquake, for an angel of the Lord descended from heaven and came and rolled back the stone and sat on it.

—Matthew 28:1–2

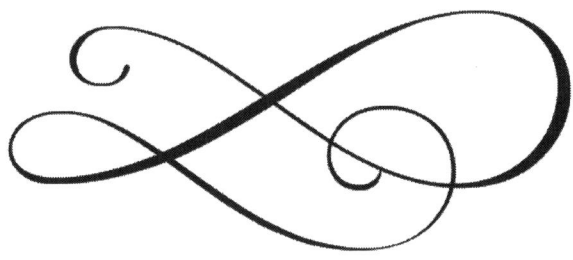

For full story:
Matthew 28:1–7

What an assignment! Roll away the stone. With pleasure!

I wanted to make a grand entrance. I could not come in my full appearance, but what I could reveal was still enough to strike healthy fear in those little guards. Ha! Guards! Against me? I appeared almost in my full glory which was enough. One look at me and they fell as though I had slain them. I then rolled back their so-called large stone—adding a little rumble of the ground for special effect—and hopped on top.

How great this felt after all that we angels have had to watch. That the Son lowered himself to take on flesh and come to this earth as an infant was in itself unnerving to observe. This is God the Son making himself appear lower than ourselves. Then to sit by while the Enemy tempted him in the wilderness—that was galling. We wanted so much to come down and do battle right then. But we were kept back. We watched his journeys about in that land, saw his sorrow and weariness. What was this all leading to? Imagine our horror when we heard him tell his followers that he was heading to his death.

Death? The Son of God die? He spoke of how these small human creatures would beat him and then kill him. How could he let that happen? But he did. I watched him in that garden; I saw the agony he suffered. Why would he not let us come down then and wipe out his enemies? Why go to the cross? I know, I know—he said that he would rise again, but the suffering and death was far more real at the time. But that time is over! Now life is real! I am not here to free my Lord. He is up and gone. I am just the messenger.

I knew that the women would soon arrive. It occurred to me that I was going to have to tone down my appearance. I could not have them fainting on me like the big bad guards. Another angel joined me. We decided to

The Angel at the Tomb

move inside. The darkness inside might dim our brightness enough to make us seem more human. Even so, the women were more than a little startled when they saw us. Apparently we were still dazzling to their eyes. My goodness, how will they ever get adjusted to glory?

I spoke up when the women came in. "Do not be afraid." (We always have to say that.) "I know you are seeking Jesus, but why? Why seek the living among the dead?" (A creative line, if I may say so.) "He is not here." (I spread my arms in a grand gesture over the area where the body would have been laid.) "He is risen!"

They just stared at me with their mouths open. "I am talking about Jesus; you know, the one you saw crucified." (You would have thought they had no clue what I was talking about.) "He is not here because he has risen just as he said that he would. Remember?"

I still wasn't quite sure if I was getting through to them. I was expecting a bit more enthusiasm. But I needed to get through the whole message.

"Go tell the disciples. Jesus plans to meet them back in Galilee. Ok? So out, out. Go quickly now. Don't forget to tell Peter and the other disciples."

I learned later that the women did actually tell the disciples at some point. They seemed to me too shaken up to be depended on. Jesus met them on the road back, and he no doubt got them on track. Maybe he was watching my interaction with them and thought reinforcement was needed.

I am not sure what to make of it all. It's not like Jesus had not prepared them for the event. He had told them several times that he would be turned over to be beaten, then crucified, and then rise from the dead. What could be clearer? I understand how difficult it is to get past the suffering and dying part, but that is all over. Jesus is alive!

Maybe I should have met them outside the tomb. I could have started off reminding them what Jesus has taught them about rising from the dead and then led them inside. They certainly were not prepared for that empty tomb.

I might be tempted to credit their shock to being women, who, I have been told, can be more emotionally impacted, but then the men were no better. They thought the women were crazy. Why, may I ask, is it so difficult to believe in angels? One of the disciples had the nerve to say about the women, "They came back saying that they had even seen a vision of angels, who said that he was alive." A vision? There was no vision about it. My partner and I were standing right in front of these women. You would say "in the flesh," but only our Lord can make that claim. Even so, we were very real in our way of being.

And even then, the disciple says, "We don't know what to make of it." Really? You don't know what to make of the message I gave? Was it complicated? I came from the presence of God to deliver his message that what the Lord had said would come true did actually come true. What is so difficult to believe? And if you are not going to believe an angel, then whom? I know now how the angel felt when Zechariah wouldn't believe his message.

I suppose their incredulity is why Jesus needed to move up the schedule of making his own appearance. These guys would never have made it to Galilee on their own. How are they going to carry on the work they are called to do—to bear witness of Jesus' resurrection?

You know, it is not like resurrection is an unknown concept. The Jews look to the resurrection of the last day. That is their hope. Why should it be incredible for their Lord to be the firstfruits of the resurrection? They hear him tell Martha that he is the resurrection and the life. Now that his resurrection has occurred, why should it be so hard to believe?

Wait a minute. I've thought of a better way that I should have made my announcement. I have with me a host of angels, like that angel had when he was sent to the shepherds. They break out into that glorious doxology. Here's the scene. I roll the stone and maybe hover over it. I give my complete message, and instead of my partner, a host of angels appear in the sky. How's this for a doxology?

> To him who sits on the throne and to the Lamb
> be blessing and honor and glory and might forever
> and ever!

I like it. I'll run it by the archangel in charge of the music for the throne room. Maybe he can use it in the worship service.

Christ is risen! He is risen, indeed! What a great assignment!

Mary Magdalene

But Mary stood weeping outside the tomb, and as she wept she stooped to look into the tomb. And she saw two angels in white, sitting where the body of Jesus had lain, one at the head and one at the feet. They said to her, "Woman, why are you weeping?" She said to them, "They have taken away my Lord, and I do not know where they have laid him."

—John 20:11–13

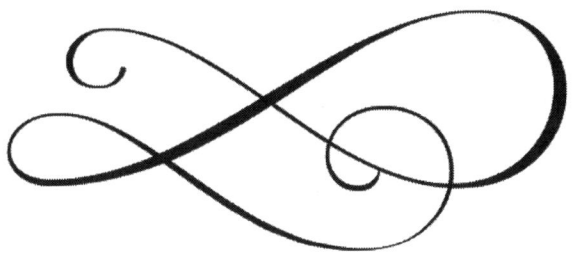

For full story:
John 20:1–18; Luke 8:1–3

Why did I go? Because I loved him. It is as simple as that. Peter had warned me and the other women not to go. There might be danger, he said. Jesus' enemies might be looking now for his followers. Besides, what could we do? We ourselves had seen the stone rolled across the entrance to the tomb.

But we had to go. I had to anyhow. I loved him. He had saved me. He had called out seven demons—seven! I had not known there could be more than one, but what I had known, what I had experienced was terrible enough. The nightmares were literally maddening. I felt the horror and apparently became a horror to others. I wanted to die. Somehow, somewhere—I don't even know how I came before him—he appeared in front of me. I heard a voice as from far away. The voice came nearer. It was his voice. He was looking at me but speaking to someone else. He was giving a command. "Come out of her!" I felt a convulsion. I heard my own voice screaming. And then quiet, all was quiet inside of me. His face that had been angry was now compassionate. "Woman, you are made clean. Go in peace." I fell at his feet and wept.

Jesus saved me from my demons, and I followed him. Several of us women followed him. Each of us had been healed in some way—some from demons like myself, others from illnesses, even leprosy. We were not strictly disciples. Jesus had not called us to follow him as disciples, and yet, follow him we did, just as they. We listened to every word he spoke, and I dare say we learned as much as the others, even as much as the Twelve. Without boasting, we were of more practical help. A number of us provided for them out of our own means.

We were different from the disciples, one difference being that we were women and they men. But there was another difference. We had each been healed by the Teacher. Jesus had saved each one of us from some kind of physical malady. It was that healing that compelled us to follow. It was not out of some ambition to be officers of a king. We believed he was the Messiah, but we were not looking for a new political kingdom. We had been healed, and we simply wanted to be near our healer, our Savior.

For he had saved us from more than physical distress. He had saved us from our inner troubles, the emotional demons that had wreaked havoc on us and had oppressed us. Release from physical ailments had helped, yes, but there was more to it. The way he spoke to us, treated us—a peace emanated from him that touched us. He healed us somehow from our past and present wounds.

We were safe with Jesus. He treated us as no other man did. We never felt degraded. We never felt like second-class citizens. We felt respect. We felt a love that was pure, that had no conditions. Who has ever loved as Jesus has loved?

And so I loved him, and I thought that I would follow him until the day I died. But he died first. Oh, I can remember now how he warned us that the day would come when he would be delivered over to his enemies and be killed. None of us could believe such a thing. It was too horrible to contemplate.

But the nightmare unfolded in front of my eyes—the scourging, the beatings, the long, horrible march outside the city. And then the horror of hanging on that cross. I was there. I never deserted him. I wept beside his mother.

He startled me when he cried out, "My God, my God, why have you forsaken me!" I knew what he had said, even as others foolishly thought he was crying out to Elijah. I wanted to call out to him that I had not forsaken him. I was still with him.

And I followed him as he was carried to his tomb. I stood with the other women a little way off as Joseph and Nicodemus prepared his body. I watched them take the body inside the tomb and then had servants roll the large stone of the entrance, sealing the body out of sight, sealing him away from me.

I had to go back to him as soon as I was allowed after the Sabbath day. I came with the other women with our spices. Yes, yes, I know—what were we thinking we would do? I don't know. We had to do something. The stone was rolled away. I ran back to tell the disciples. Peter and John ran to the tomb, found it empty, and then walked away. They walked away! How could they leave?

I stood alone weeping outside the tomb. I peered in again. There were two men dressed in white inside. They asked why I was weeping. My grief doubled. Two men had walked away; two ask why I am weeping, as though surprised by it.

"They have taken away my Lord, and I do not know where they have laid him. Can no one understand? Can no one help me?"

And then another man—I cannot see him clearly:

"Woman, why are you weeping? Whom are you seeking?"

It was like one of my nightmares of old. No one makes sense. There is an empty tomb, my Lord is missing, and no one cares!

Maybe the man takes care of the garden.

"Sir, if you have carried him away, tell me where you have laid him, and I will take him away."

No, I was not making sense, but neither was anyone else. Where is the body? Where is my Lord? I have always been with him. Where is he?

"Mary."

I know that voice. I know that love.

"Rabboni!"

My dear Teacher. He came back. He came back for me.

I fell on my knees and clung to him. He was alive. He was with me.

"Do not cling to me, for I have not yet ascended to the Father; but go to my brothers and say to them, 'I am ascending to my Father and your Father, to my God and your God.'"

I did not understand fully what he was saying about ascending. What I could understand was that he was standing, in the flesh, in front of me.

And I understood his order. I did not want to leave him but I must obey. And so I ran back to Peter and John and the other disciples, and told them how Jesus had appeared to me.

Except for John, they did not believe me. Marked it up to female hysteria. I know what I have seen, what I have heard, and what I have touched. My Lord is alive. He is risen from the dead. I need never fear being abandoned.

> I have trusted in your steadfast love;
>   my heart shall rejoice in your salvation.
> I will sing to the LORD,
>   because he has dealt bountifully with me.

Cleopas

That very day two of them were going to a village named Emmaus, about seven miles from Jerusalem, and they were talking with each other about all these things that had happened. While they were talking and discussing together, Jesus himself drew near and went with them. But their eyes were kept from recognizing him.

—Luke 24:13–16

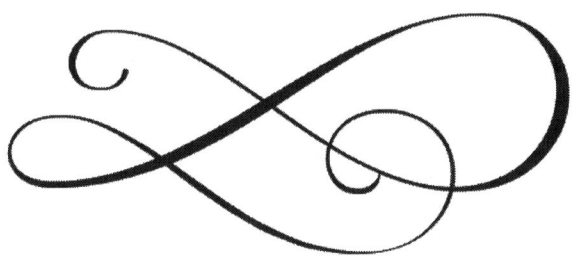

For full story:
Luke 24:13–35

Sometimes one's eyes must be closed for the mind to be opened. That is how I understand what happened to me and my brother. How else could we have not recognized our Lord unless our eyes had been veiled? Indeed, how could we not have recognized his voice? And yet there we were, walking along with him, listening to him teach as he had done so many times before, and he was but a stranger to us.

We were heading to Emmaus, I'm not even sure why. Those were gloomy, even despairing days. We had followed Jesus of Nazareth, a man who was a prophet mighty in deed and word, so mighty that we dared to believe he was the Messiah who would redeem Israel. What more wonders could the Messiah have done? He healed the sick, he cast out demons, he multiplied food, he calmed storms; he even raised the dead to life! Everyone was ready to crown him king; everyone would have followed him—everyone but the leaders who killed him.

And now he was dead. Perhaps he could have been made a martyr, but they not only killed him, they crucified him, and so he was cursed, for our law says that whoever is hanged upon a tree is cursed by God. Who then could claim him as Messiah or anyone sent from God? No, it was all over, except that—not that we were really believing it—on the third day of his death some of our women had rushed to where we were hiding claiming that they had seen angels at our Lord's tomb who announced that Jesus was alive! Some of the men checked it out. His body was missing but no angels. Not to dismiss the women, but we all know how they can be taken away by emotions.

So, we are telling the stranger all this, and he surprises us with his own emotional response. "O foolish ones, and slow of heart to believe all that the prophets have spoken!" As soon as he said "O foolish ones," I should have picked up on who he was. He had used those words and tone more than once with us.

He then asked his rhetorical question to begin his lesson: "Was it not necessary that the Messiah should suffer these things and enter into his glory?" With that he took us on a wondrous journey through the Scriptures of Moses and the Prophets.

"Don't you see at the very beginning in God's curse on the Serpent? The Seed of Eve will be bruised and yet will crush the head of Satan."

"Cursed on the tree? Of course! That's the whole point of the crucifixion—to fulfill the law. The Messiah must take the curse of his people. The curse must fall upon him if he is to save them."

"Now let's look at the Passover. The Messiah is the Passover Lamb who causes death to pass over his people. The Passover meal is the meal of the new covenant that the Messiah mediates as he delivers his people through the Red Sea of judgment."

"Do you see now the meaning of the scapegoat on the Day of Atonement? The sins and the curse of the people are laid upon the Messiah who carries them away."

"The Messiah is the one to whom Isaiah is referring as the Suffering Servant."

> "The Messiah was pierced for your transgressions;
>   he was crushed for your iniquities;
>   upon him was the chastisement that brought you peace,
>   and with his wounds you are healed."

He showed us references to the Messiah's resurrection.

"It was of the Messiah that David wrote, 'you will not abandon my soul to Hades'."

"Did Jesus not tell you to look to Jonah for the sign of his resurrection?"

He pointed us beyond the resurrection to the Messiah's ascension into glory.

"Lift up your heads, O gates…that the King of glory may come in."

"Look at the sacrificial system. It foreshadows the all-sufficient sacrifice of the Messiah for his people.… The High Priest represents how the Messiah became the great High Priest offering sacrifice and prayers… Have you never thought about who Melchizedek was that Abraham would give a tithe to him?… What do you think Abraham really meant when he told his son, Isaac, that God would provide a sacrifice?… Then there is Boaz who serves as kinsman-redeemer, and Hosea who ransoms his wife back… Think of what the real inheritance of Israel is. Think of the real Promised Land, of the heavenly Jerusalem."

Step after step, teaching after teaching—our hearts were burning within us. Perhaps we were so caught up in the teaching that we didn't think about who it was doing the teaching. With every lesson from the Scriptures, the dots began to connect, and we could see where we had gone wrong. We were looking for a political Messiah to redeem Israel when the Scriptures had been pointing to a spiritual Messiah to redeem the heart of Israel. And even Israel was a misunderstanding. We assumed the Messiah had only the interests of our nation, our people in mind. But he showed us the Scripture passages where all the nations come to be blessed.

> All the ends of the earth shall remember
>   and turn to the LORD,
> and all the families of the nations
>   shall worship before you.
> For kingship belongs to the LORD,
>   and he rules over the nations.

The Messiah is the Messiah for a people from every nation and tongue and tribe. That is why the good news must go out to the ends of the earth.

We lost track of the time and distance arriving at the village. It was near evening. The stranger made as if he were going further, but we urged him to stay with us at our friend's house and to have dinner with us. We wanted as much time with him and his teaching as we could get. In deference we asked him to give the blessing over the food. He stood, took the bread and blessed and broke it and gave it to us. It was then that our eyes were opened, and we recognized our Lord from his final meal with us. But before we could speak to him, he vanished. If he had merely appeared and then vanished, we would have credited it to an apparition, but we had spent a whole journey with him feeding on his teaching.

We ran back to Jerusalem to tell the rest of the disciples. They had news for us—that Peter had seen the Lord. As we talked excitedly, there he was! Jesus! Our Lord! "Peace to you!" he said. We could have jumped out of our skins! This time he ate with us, but even more exciting, he continued to teach. He continued to open our eyes and our minds to "thus it is written."

He pointed out that he was only telling us what he had been teaching all along, how everything written about him in the Law of Moses and the Prophets and the Psalms must be fulfilled. He had taught these things before, but it was now, after his resurrection, that we had ears to hear. It was after his resurrection that what we did not want to hear—about his suffering and death—began to make sense. I remember how we were afraid to ask questions whenever he would refer to his death, how Peter even tried to stop him from speaking of it.

That evening, our Lord not only spoke, but he showed us the marks on his hands and feet. He wanted to show clearly that he had flesh and bones. But he was also showing yet again how Scripture had been fulfilled—"they have pierced my hands and feet."

And so we now become the witnesses that he intended for us to become. We are to bear witness of his life, his sufferings and death, his resurrection, and his ascension. Our eyes are opened and now our minds are opened to understand what these things all mean, how they are the fulfillment of what was written in the Law of Moses, in the Prophets, and in the Psalms. The Messiah has come as was promised in the Scriptures.

Thomas

Now Thomas, one of the Twelve, called the Twin, was not with them when Jesus came. So the other disciples told him, "We have seen the Lord." But he said to them, "Unless I see in his hands the mark of the nails, and place my finger into the mark of the nails, and place my hand into his side, I will never believe."

—John 20:24–25

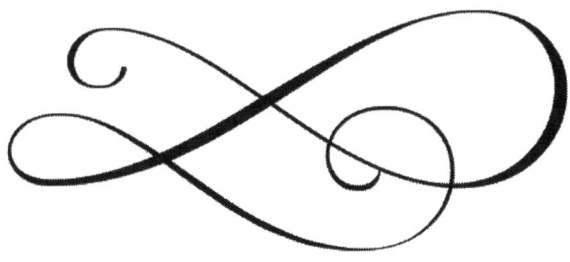

For full story:
John 20:24–29

I saw my Lord. I saw the mark of the nails in his hands. I saw the wound in his side where he had been pierced, and I believed. No, I did not place my finger in the mark of the nails or my hand into his side. It was enough to simply see my Lord to believe. It is to my shame that it took so much.

I have never thought of myself as a skeptic so much as being a person who valued clear thinking and clear speech. I looked with faith for the prophesied Messiah, and I followed Jesus with the thought that he might very well be that Messiah. It was his power that he displayed, which, as a rational Jew who looked for signs, I regarded as demonstration that he could be the one. But then, there were things that did not compute. The signs pointed to the Messiah of power that we were looking for, but Jesus wasn't following script.

For one thing, he didn't use his miracles in a way I could understand. Really, by the time of his entering into Jerusalem he ought to have had more than a few dozen disciples following him, and, quite frankly, something a bit more organized into a military unit. I thought we were to be re-establishing the kingdom of God and kicking out the Romans.

Maybe the Messiah didn't need an army, but his teaching about the kingdom was vague. Those parables never were clear. Jesus explained that he told parables to keep their meaning hidden from those without "ears to hear," but I'm not sure if we disciples had ears to hear. When we were bold enough, we would ask him to explain them, but as often as not we just nodded our heads, all the more puzzled.

Not to be critical of my brethren, but grasping figures of speech was not their strong point. Teacher spoke of leaven of the Pharisees, and they thought he was scolding them for forgetting to bring bread. He referred to dying Lazarus as falling asleep, and they couldn't understand why Jesus needed to go wake him up. I wish I was remembered for what I said then: "Let us also go, that we might die with him." But then, after running away in Gethsemane, it might be best to forget that little expression of bravado.

What I am trying to do is explain my foolish obstinacy after my brethren attested to seeing our risen Lord. I got carried away, I know. "Unless I see in his hands the mark of the nails, and place my finger into the mark of the nails, and place my hand into his side, I will never believe." A bit theatrical, but by this time I was fed up with their credulity and their dullness of thinking.

Proclaim him what they might—Son of God, the Messiah—they were just as confused as I as to who our Teacher was. They were just as befuddled by his teachings. And none of us understood his references to suffering and to dying and to rising. I was the only one to call Jesus on this. It was the very night of his arrest. He is going away, he tells us. "And if I go and prepare a place for you, I will come again and will take you to myself, that where I am you may be also. And you know the way to where I am going."

Well, no, we don't know where you are going. We don't know what you are talking about. How can we know the way? I had to say it. No one else would. The only one who ever spoke up was Peter but never to ask, only to spurt out something ridiculous. Did the man ever think before speaking? Did he ever think?

Even then Jesus gives an obscure answer: "I am the way, the truth, and the life. No one comes to the Father except through me. If you had known me, you would have known my Father also. From now on you do know him and have seen him." That leads to another long vague discourse, at the end of which, the rest of the disciples say, "Ah, now you are speaking plainly and not using figurative speech! Now we know that you know all things and do not need anyone to question you; this is why we believe that you came from God."

Give me a break! They had no idea what he was talking about. It just sounded deep and mysterious, which must mean that Teacher is from God. I believed Jesus was from God in some way. But what I wanted was clear teaching. I wanted explanation. If we see him, we see the Father. He can't send us the Comforter if he doesn't go away. And all we need to do is to believe in him. Believe in him about what?

Then he was gone. If he had simply vanished, then maybe I would have believed something. But he didn't leave us; he was taken from us. He didn't rise up in the air to the Father to prepare us rooms in some heavenly mansion; he was arrested, tried as a criminal, and nailed on a cross. What were we to believe in now? Where was the Comforter now that the Teacher was gone?

We hid. We all ran away the very same night we vowed to die with him. We were nothing but cowards. The truth was pushed in front of our faces—our Teacher was nothing more than a man. We certainly had clarity about that.

I left the group the second day. I needed to get away. When I did return the next evening, everyone was excited. "We have seen the Lord! The doors were locked, and suddenly he was standing among us."

Shouldn't I have believed them? What more evidence did I need than their eye-witness? I could have used the testimony of better witnesses, not a bunch of credulous, uneducated men wanting desperately to believe in their Teacher. In the highly strung state we were all in, it was easier to believe that they had worked themselves up to see Jesus whom we all loved. Did anyone touch him? Could anyone attest that he was of real flesh? No? Then I would not believe until I placed my finger into the mark of the nails and placed my hand into his side.

I felt smug and certainly superior to my brothers and the women there. I alone was the disciple not to give way to emotion. I alone was the clear thinker. I was not a skeptic. All I demanded was rational evidence. Let Jesus appear before me and submit himself to me for testing.

He did not come back. Not the next night or the night after that. My smugness grew as the confidence of the disciples waned. Most of them—some still clung tenaciously to their belief in Jesus' resurrection.

Eight nights later, the doors locked, Jesus appears in front of us all. "Peace be with you," he says, and then he turns to me, holding out his hands and pulling aside his robe so I could see his side: "Put your finger here, and see my hands; and put out your hand, and place it in my side. Do not disbelieve, but believe."

I fell on my knees. I fell on my knees—in shame? In worship! For the veil over my befuddled, obstinate mind was removed. My Teacher was my Lord and my God. Yes, my God, for in seeing my Lord I was seeing God my Father. The Way, the Truth, and the Life stood before me in full clarity.

Now that I could see with my eyes and touch if I had dared, then I believed in my Lord and my God. Yes, what a fool, for I missed all along what he had been teaching, what he had desired most from us—to believe in him when we don't have it all understood; to believe in him without the proof we demand; to trust what he had told us clearly—that he would suffer, that he would die, and that he would rise again.

"Blessed are those who have not seen and yet have believed." How more wonderful it would have been if I had believed my fellow disciples. How more meaningful if I had trusted in those darkest hours before the resurrection that my Lord would keep his word and rise. How more precious would it have been if I had expected to see him again. How beautiful it would have been for him to say to me, "Thomas, blessed are you because you did not see when the others did and yet you believed."

My Lord has blessed me. Even so, to be faithful in having faith and keeping faith—that is blessing indeed.

Peter

When they had finished breakfast, Jesus said to Simon Peter, "Simon, son of John, do you love me more than these?" He said to him, "Yes, Lord; you know that I love you." He said to him, "Feed my lambs."

—John 21:15

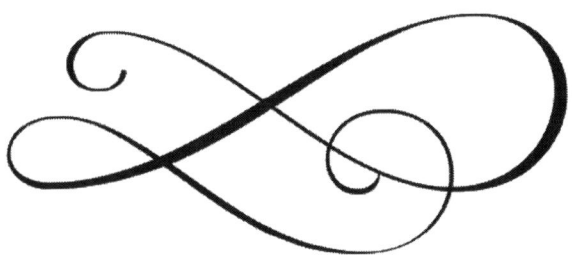

For full story:
John 21:1–19

I did love him. I knew that he knew I loved him when he was asking. I knew there was more behind the question. Three times he asked me. Yes, I know; three times I had denied him. Was he rubbing in the denials? That is not his way. Jesus had never before been reluctant to confront me with my… impulsiveness.

"O you of little faith, why did you doubt?"

"Get behind me, Satan! You are a hindrance to me. For you are not setting your mind on the things of God, but on the things of man."

"This is my beloved Son, with whom I am well pleased; listen to him." That was from his Father.

"If I do not wash you, you have no share with me."

"Truly, I tell you, this very night, before the rooster crows, you will deny me three times."

Three times. Not once, not twice, but I denied my Lord three times, just as he said I would.

How could I believe him? I loved him. I knew that I loved him more than my own life. I knew that my declaration to die for him was sincere, and I would have died for him if…if he had allowed me. But when he commanded me to put my sword down in my effort to defend him, I did not know what to do then. I did not understand him. Now I see it, but not then.

I had never understood why he had reacted so violently when I first defended him against himself. I had confessed that he was the Messiah. He seemed so pleased. He was going to build his Church and the gates of hell would not prevail. The hearts of us all were stirred, but then he began to talk about his defeat—how the religious leaders were going to get the best of him; he would suffer, even die. Yes, he said that he would rise again, but what did that even mean? I knew what suffering and death meant. I had to say something. Ha! I always have to say something.

And so again, that last night with us, he speaks of betrayal and abandonment. No, no, no! It was one thing to talk about what his enemies would do, but now us? His disciples who loved him most? Who had followed him everywhere? I know, he spoke of rising again even then, but who could listen after he had accused us of such spineless behavior?

I run away? I could be accused of being a fool, but a coward? When my Lord was in need? How could he even suggest such a thing? And so my words of bravado. But I still contest that I would have died for him if it had been his will. I remember everything he had said after that "Get behind me Satan" remark. He said, " For whoever would save his life will lose it, but whoever loses his life for my sake will find it."

I was ready from then on to lose my life for his sake. And when I acted to do so, he rebuked me for the last time. "Put your sword into its sheath; shall I not drink the cup that the Father has given me?"

We looked at each other, but briefly, for he turned to his captors and walked away with them. I ran but not far. John and I stood at the edge of the garden and then followed behind. The rest of my shame is known. I could not simply deny I knew him; I had to call down a curse on myself, so vehement was my denial. A curse should have fallen on me. The cock crowed; I remembered Jesus' words; and again I ran, this time in shame with bitter tears.

The next time I would run would be to the empty tomb. Mary Magdalene told us that he had risen and that she had spoken to him. I ran to the tomb, found it empty, and wondered what had happened. Why could I not believe he had risen? Why must I fail yet once again to believe my Lord?

Everything Jesus said had come true. He suffered under the hands of elders and priests; he was killed; and he rose from the dead, even on the third day; even that he would meet us in Galilee. I should have known instantly it was he when he told us to cast our net on the other side of the boat. Had he not instructed us do the same thing when we first met? John recognized first what was happening. He always did. He understood the meaning of the empty tomb before I. And he was the only one of us who could bear to watch our Lord crucified. John…but I digress.

The net bulged as we tugged. That first wonder when it had happened long ago came to me. At that time I was filled with fear at who this Jesus of Nazareth must be. "Depart from me, for I am a sinful man, O Lord"—maybe my only sane words I've blurted out, other than the confession of his Messiahship. Little then did I understand how true my words were about me. I should have said such about me when he said that I would deny him.

But I was not thinking of sin that second time on a boat. I was not thinking about me. My Lord and my Savior was on the shore, and I had to get to him. And what was he doing? Cooking fish. What profound words did he have to say? Bring more fish and have some breakfast. It was as though no great miracle had taken place—no miraculous catch; no miraculous resurrection. We were Jesus and his disciples once again on the shore of the Galilean Sea eating together.

What else to expect? He had already appeared to us twice, but then he would slip away. He was different somehow: more distant even as he was near; more unearthly though he ate a meal; teaching us as before about the kingdom of God, but now about how he had fulfilled what the Scriptures foretold.

I listened intently to everything he said. I would not be such a fool again. I listened, but with unsettled heart. I had thought I was the best of the disciples, the leader closest to our Lord. It was I who first confessed his true identity, I upon whose confession his Church was to be built, a church against which hell could not prevail. It was I…it was I alone who three times denied him, who even called down curses upon my head. Was I cursed? If not rejected outright, was I so disgraced to lose my place of leadership? Was that not already passed over to John, he who most proved himself to be trustworthy?

"Feed my sheep." Three times Jesus asked if I loved him; three times he exhorted me to tend and feed his sheep, his lambs. But what of my sin? He had already dealt with my sin on the cross. That is why he would not let me die for him; he must die for me. The curse I called upon my own head? It fell upon his. And as he did not depart from this poor sinful man years ago, so he would not depart now, as he commissioned me to go forth. As a fisher of men? Yes, but also as a shepherd. I now am to be a good shepherd who tends the flock of my Good Shepherd.

I am to follow the ways of my Shepherd who had come to lay down his life for his sheep. He left me with a promise—some day I would have that privilege to lay down my life for my Lord. May he keep me faithful.

Matthew

Now the eleven disciples went to Galilee, to the mountain to which Jesus had directed them. And when they saw him they worshiped him, but some doubted. And Jesus came and said to them, "All authority in heaven and on earth has been given to me. Go therefore and make disciples of all nations, baptizing them in the name of the Father and of the Son and of the Holy Spirit, teaching them to observe all that I have commanded you. And behold, I am with you always, to the end of the age."

—Matthew 28:16–20

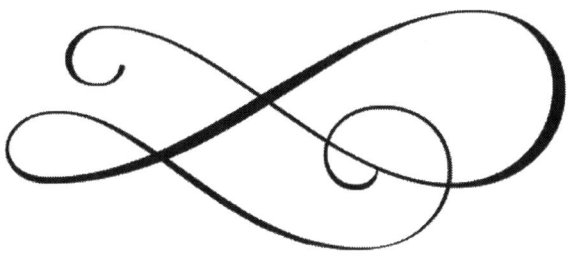

For full story:
Matthew 9:9–13

"Follow me," he said, and so I did. Nothing complicated, really. Perhaps it was boredom that prompted me, perhaps disillusionment. Perhaps it was just time. I had heard of Jesus, and then I witnessed his teaching and his miracles. He lived in the city I worked in as a tax collector. My friends joked about him at our parties, yet not with the same sarcasm they typically jested in. There was something unique about this traveling rabbi—an authority, a sincerity absent from the other religious leaders.

"Follow me," as though that should be the natural thing for me to do. Get up from my collection booth in public and join his disciples—me, the despised tax collector and sinner. Follow the rabbi as though I were another religious student devoted to God. And so I did. I turned the booth over to an assistant, walked after him, and never left him afterwards.

Before the day was over, I invited him to my home for one last evening with my friends. And he accepted. He accepted the invitation of a sinner as though that should be the natural thing for him to do. He, the holy man of God, entered the home of a sinner, the guest at a party of the city's public sinners.

All of my friends came, none who would have entered a synagogue even if they had been allowed in. All of them came eagerly, perhaps some for entertainment, but all respectful and all listening to him. He spoke to us as though we were friends, as though we were disciples wanting to hear his favorite topic—the kingdom of God.

The only ones who saw the incongruity of the episode were the Pharisees, at least they were the ones who complained. I suspect Jesus' disciples were a bit uncomfortable with the setting they found themselves in. But the Pharisees expressed what even we sinners acknowledged was so odd—that the teacher was dining with tax collectors and sinners.

I did hear Jesus' response. "Those who are well have no need of a physician, but those who are sick. Go and learn what this means, 'I desire mercy, and not sacrifice.' For I came not to call the righteous, but sinners."

That is what he had done regarding me. He had called me, a sinner, to follow him. Something inside of me responded. It is that simple. He called me, not overlooking who I was, but because of who I was. My sinful condition aroused in him mercy instead of wrath. Is that why I did what was for me the most outrageous thing I could do, which was to follow him?

"Follow me." I followed him everywhere he went. I witnessed his miracles; I listened to his teachings. I shared in his daily life, watching how he interacted with persons on every level of society. I assisted him in his ministry and was sent out with the other disciples on short-term mission trips. On those trips even I was granted the power to heal and to cast out demons.

I followed him in his success. I followed him when hounded by the religious authorities. I followed him as far as Gethsemane. I followed him until I abandoned him in his hour of need, just as he said I and the other disciples would do.

We did not abandon one another but hid together in our fear, our shame, and our despair. And so I was with them when Jesus came to us. He came to us as though that should be the most natural thing to happen. "Shalom," he greeted us, as though he was coming to a dinner to which he had been invited.

The next forty days we met again often as he taught the significance of his suffering and resurrection. Most of that teaching had to do with how he had fulfilled the prophecies and teachings of the Scriptures. For me, the most memorable time was on the mountain back in Galilee. We had met there at his bidding. It was there that he gave us our commission.

> All authority in heaven and on earth has been given to me.
> Go therefore and make disciples of all nations, baptizing
> them in the name of the Father and of the Son and of
> the Holy Spirit, teaching them to observe all that I have
> commanded you. And behold, I am with you always, to
> the end of the age.

No longer would we be told to come. The time has arrived for us to answer the call to go. We are to call others to follow, to become disciples with us—to baptize and to teach, to do the work that our Lord did among us. As he made disciples, so are we to do. The difference, of course, is that we call others to be disciples not of us but of him, to follow him.

We are to call people wherever they are and whoever they are. Call them from their homes, from their places of work, from their places of play. We are to call sinners and even the self-proclaimed righteous. We are to call the rich and the poor, the powerful and the oppressed. We are to proclaim Jesus in the temple courts of Jerusalem and in the cities and villages throughout the empire. We are to go everywhere we can, even if it should cost us our lives.

He did warn of this and of suffering. "If anyone would come after me, let him deny himself and take up his cross and follow me." We will each take up our cross, to be sure. If the Master should be persecuted, so should his followers expect the same.

Will we abandon the task? May the Lord grant us grace to stay the course. I believe we will. For wherever we go and whatever should happen, our Lord will be with us. That is his promise, and he will keep it. He will keep us true to him.

And he has promised reward. Indeed, we shall sit on twelve thrones, judging the twelve tribes of Israel. I, for good reason regarded a traitor to my country, will sit upon a throne. I became a tax collector to get rich. I left the money to follow Jesus. I am now promised riches beyond what I could have imagined. To tell the truth, saving my soul is reward enough. I will gladly lose my life for my Lord's sake, if it means finding and keeping my soul; if it means dwelling in the kingdom of heaven with my Savior.

It is to that kingdom my hope is founded. To live in it, to serve in it. To be found worthy of it. To be called to recline at table with Abraham, Isaac, and Jacob in it. I cannot understand why such a hope should be granted to me, a sinner, who had chosen to serve my country's oppressors. The Pharisees were right to condemn me. Jesus would have been right to do so, as well. Yet, he chose mercy, even the mercy to follow him.

"Follow me." How natural such an unnatural call and unnatural response seemed at the time. How natural such an unnatural commission seemed then on that mountain. We are as unlikely a group to succeed as we were individuals to receive a call from Jesus in the first place to follow him. Perhaps the simple answer lies in Jesus himself. No one else would we follow. No one else would we obey the command to go forth. But then, no one else could make the promise he has made—to be with us always, to the end of the age.

What else can I do but follow him?

CONCLUSION

HE WAS LIFTED ON HIGH

The Angel of the Ascension

And when he had said these things, as they were looking on, he was lifted up, and a cloud took him out of their sight. And while they were gazing into heaven as he went, behold, two men stood by them in white robes, and said, "Men of Galilee, why do you stand looking into heaven? This Jesus, who was taken up from you into heaven, will come in the same way as you saw him go into heaven."

—Acts 1:9–11

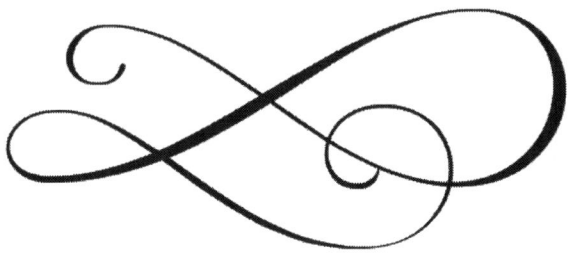

For full story:
Acts 1:6–11

It is a wondrous sight—Jesus rising into the air on a cloud that took him out of the sight of his disciples. Their necks were craned and their mouths gaping wide. There was wonder in their eyes, wonder and grief, for this spectacular ascension was their Lord's final departure.

Even after he could not be seen, they continued to gaze into the sky. They did not lower their eyes until we spoke to them—my fellow angel and I. We came to them with one message—Jesus will return. Just as they saw him taken up on a cloud, so he will descend once more again on a cloud.

It is a message they needed to hear. As heartening and instructive it had been for Jesus to meet with them over the forty days after his resurrection, such time together made them feel that he would never leave. Surely that had been their hope. We heard his final discourse with his disciples. They asked him, "Lord, will you at this time restore the kingdom to Israel?" That was not an academic inquiry; it was a hope-filled question. Perhaps soon, even now, the consummation of the kingdom would take place. That is what they have longed for. That is what they want to participate in.

They want to reign beside Jesus in that kingdom. They want to see him glorified before all the world. They want him to display his power. They had hoped to see it in his ministry. The miracles stirred up that hope. The entry into Jerusalem—was this to be the time? Then came the arrest and the crucifixion. The hope is dashed but then resurrected with their Lord's resurrection, the greatest miracle. Now the kingdom is to be established. But Jesus does not go public. His time is not spent in miracles but in teaching. They are wonderful teachings to be sure, showing how he had fulfilled the Scriptures, but when will Jesus restore the kingdom? When will he complete the work he had come to do?

It turns out that his work will be completed when they complete theirs. They have to first be witnesses of his resurrection and of who he is. They have to be witnesses of the gospel, of the saving work that he has indeed completed. The work of spreading the gospel is now laid upon their shoulders. They must make disciples of Jesus like themselves.

They heard this teaching, but as long as he remained with them they could not but hope that he never would actually leave. And so, as he rose before them into the sky, they saw with their own eyes that he was leaving them alone with a mission still to be completed. There was the promise that Jesus would be with them, but how much comfort could that be when they do not see him or feel him?

I suppose we helped them. We appeared as nothing more than two men: no heavenly host from the sky suddenly presented itself with a loud chorus. The message itself had to be received by faith. Of course, they did have a visual demonstration of God's power before them in the sky, but it was of a glory diminishing as it rose higher until it vanished.

Do they understand what their mission entails? Do they grasp that they too must take up a cross? Did they catch on that they too have a baptism to undergo, a cup to drink? They had not been able to hear Jesus speak of his sufferings and death; have they heard now the warnings he gave of their own sufferings and death? And when that time comes—when they must suffer—will they remain faithful to their mission?

So small, so weak they seem. They ran away before. What will keep them faithful now? What will keep them to a task far beyond their capabilities?

What was it that Jesus said to them before he ascended? Ah, yes: "You will receive power when the Holy Spirit has come upon you, and you will be my witnesses in Jerusalem and in all Judea and Samaria, and to the end of the earth."

It is not *what* will change them from deserters to faithful witnesses but *who*. "When the Holy Spirit has come." Of course! The Spirit of God—he will empower them; he will transform them. Somehow, he will make them our Lord's witnesses even as they take up their own crosses. How else could it be?

The Spirit—Jesus had promised him all along. He had tried to comfort them with the promise of the Helper that he would send. "It is to your advantage that I go away, for if I do not go away, the Helper will not come to you." I suspect that reasoning did little to comfort them. But they will find comfort from him and even power. Before the baptism of persecution will come the baptism of the Holy Spirit, and it is that baptism that will give them the boldness and the wisdom to bear witness to the saving power of the cross even as they bear their own.

And that Spirit will work in the hearts of those they are sent to make disciples of. He will do the work of conviction of sin and of giving faith. It will be the Spirit who gives life to the dead so that they can hear the gospel preached. It is the Holy Spirit who will fulfill the words of the prophet: "I will give you a new heart, and a new spirit I will put within you. And I will remove the heart of stone from your flesh and give you a heart of flesh."

Then shall the chosen of God hear the word of God. They will hear the words spoken by men but inspired by the Spirit of God.

For now, this small group of disciples wait just as they have been instructed to do. They wait and they pray and they study the Scriptures. How surprising are these human creatures. However vacillating and faltering they may be, they stand back up, they return to their Master, and they do his bidding, even if that bidding is to patiently wait.

But even that waiting is bearing fruit, for as they pray and study, the Spirit is working within them. They are growing in knowledge, growing in conviction. The teaching that Jesus gave while still with them is taking more and more hold of them. The Spirit is doing exactly what Jesus said he would do. "He will teach you all things and bring to your remembrance all that I have said to you." When the baptism of the Spirit comes upon them, they will be ready to preach the gospel.

We angels long to look into how all of this redemptive work of the Son will be played out. This small band of unlikely messengers will take the gospel message to the end of the earth. Surely, they will need the Holy Spirit. But now, we want to know—when will the power of the Holy Spirit descend upon them? And what will it do to them? Why—if I may be so bold to ask—were we not chosen to spread the gospel?

The Father knows his plans, which will be more wondrous than what we heavenly messengers can foresee. What could have been more wondrous than the coming and the work of the Son? What wonders are still to be when the Holy Spirit arrives? What will it be like as the kingdom of heaven expands upon this earth? And, yes, when will it be, what will it be like, when the Son returns? We angels long to look!

OTHER TITLES BY
D. MARION CLARK

To Know Wisdom: Meditations on Proverbs

*The Problem of Good:
When the World Seems Fine without God*, editor

Common Grace: A Primer

Biblical Precepts for Marriage

Speaking the Truth in Love

*What Matters:
The Five Most Important Spiritual Lessons I Have Learned*

The author may be reached at mg79clark@yahoo.com.

Made in the USA
Columbia, SC
05 November 2021